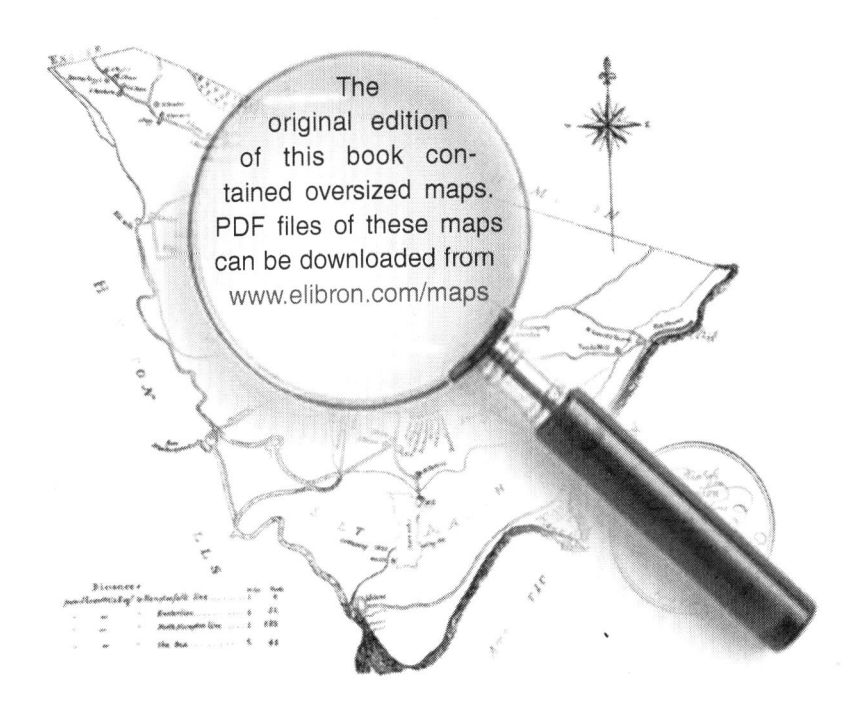

The original edition of this book contained oversized maps. PDF files of these maps can be downloaded from www.elibron.com/maps

Josiah Harlan

A MEMOIR

OF

INDIA AND AFGHANISTAN

WITH OBSERVATIONS ON THE

PRESENT EXCITING AND CRITICAL STATE

AND

FUTURE PROSPECTS OF THOSE COUNTRIES

Elibron Classics
www.elibron.com

Elibron Classics series.

© 2005 Adamant Media Corporation.

ISBN 1-4021-6365-7 (paperback)
ISBN 1-4021-5360-0 (hardcover)

This Elibron Classics Replica Edition is an unabridged facsimile of the edition published in 1842 by J. Dobson, Philadelphia.

Elibron and Elibron Classics are trademarks of Adamant Media Corporation. All rights reserved.

This book is an accurate reproduction of the original. Any marks, names, colophons, imprints, logos or other symbols or identifiers that appear on or in this book, except for those of Adamant Media Corporation and BookSurge, LLC, are used only for historical reference and accuracy and are not meant to designate origin or imply any sponsorship by or license from any third party.

A MEMOIR

OF

INDIA AND AVGHANISTAUN,

WITH OBSERVATIONS ON THE

PRESENT EXCITING AND CRITICAL STATE

AND

FUTURE PROSPECTS OF THOSE COUNTRIES.

BY J. HARLAN

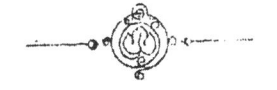

PHILADELPHIA :

J. DOBSON, 106 CHESTNUT STREET

PARIS,

GALIGNANNET C^e,	THÉOPHILE BARROIS,
RUE VIVIENNE, 18.	QUAI VOLTAIRE, 13.
STASSIN ET XAVIER,	HECTOR BOSSANGE,
RUE DU COQ, 6.	QUAI VOLTAIRE, 11.
AMYOT, RUE DE LA PAIX, 6.	TRUCHY, BOULEVARD DES ITALIENS, 18.

1842.

Ex-Ameer Dost Mahomed.

LINES ADDRESSED TO DOST MAHOMED

ON THE BATTLE FIELD OF KANDAHAR, WHEN CONTENDING WITH SHUJAH, 1834.

Stand! cried his Mentor, whither wouldst thou flee?
The ground thou stand'st on 's all the world to thee;
Thy throne the saddle, crowned by natal star—
Thou stand'st a warrior in the midst of war!
Here find a throne, or fill a hero's grave,
Where rest the houseless and the hopeless brave;
For God, the Prophet, and thy deeds of fame,
A martyr's paradise, or victor's name.

A MEMOIR

OF

INDIA AND AVGHANISTAUN,

WITH OBSERVATIONS ON THE

PRESENT EXCITING AND CRITICAL STATE

AND

FUTURE PROSPECTS OF THOSE COUNTRIES.

COMPRISING REMARKS ON THE MASSACRE OF THE BRITISH ARMY IN CABUL, BRITISH POLICY IN INDIA, A DETAILED DESCRIPTIVE CHARACTER OF DOST MAHOMED AND HIS COURT, ETC.

With an Appendix

ON THE FULFILMENT OF A TEXT OF DANIEL, IN REFERENCE TO THE PRESENT PROPHETIC CONDITION OF MAHOMEDAN NATIONS THROUGHOUT THE WORLD, AND THE SPEEDY DISSOLUTION OF THE OTTOMAN EMPIRE.

BY J. HARLAN,

LATE COUNSELLOR OF STATE, AID-DE-CAMP, AND GENERAL OF THE STAFF TO DOST MAHOMED, AMEER OF CABUL.

PHILADELPHIA:

J. DOBSON, 106 CHESTNUT STREET.
R. BALDWIN, PATERNOSTER ROW, LONDON.
H. BOSSANGE, 11 QUAI VOLTAIRE, PARIS.
1842.

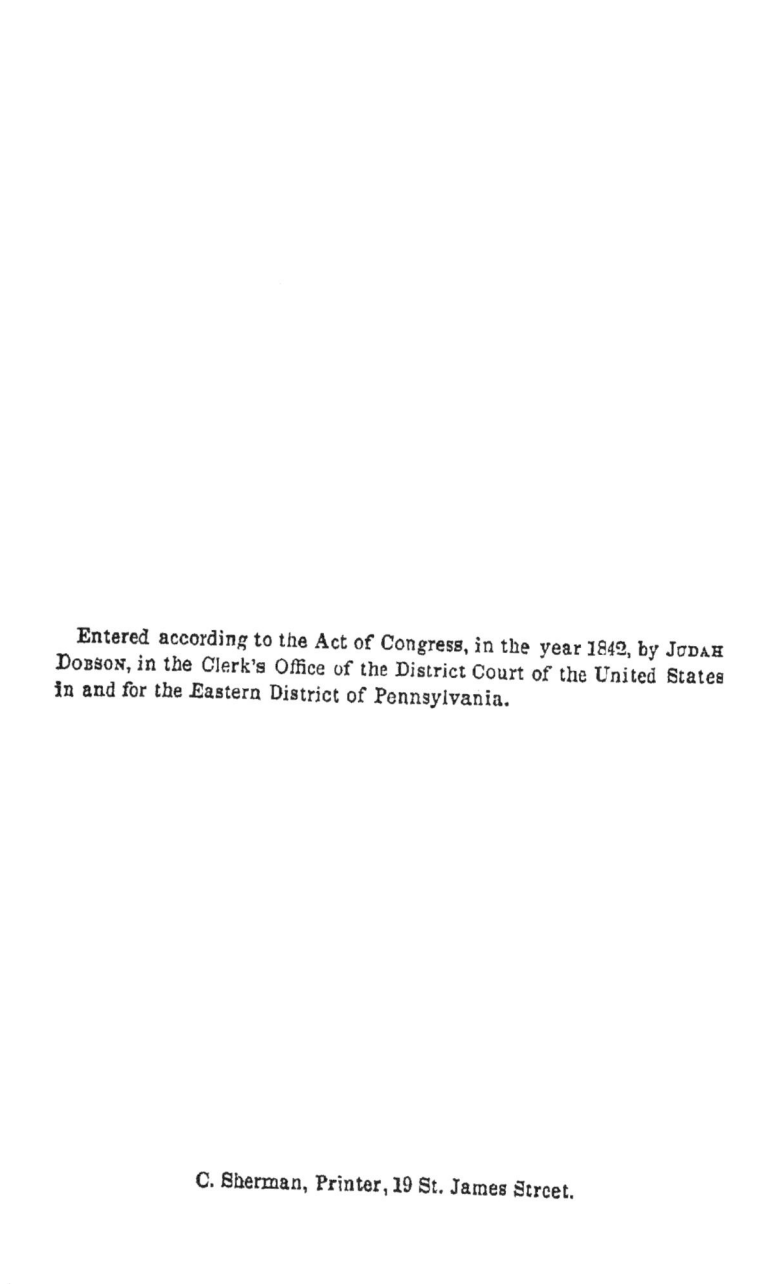

Entered according to the Act of Congress, in the year 1842, by JUDAH DOBSON, in the Clerk's Office of the District Court of the United States in and for the Eastern District of Pennsylvania.

C. Sherman, Printer, 19 St. James Street.

CONTENTS.

PREFACE.

Massacre—Whigs—American interest—Tory policy—British tenure of India—Successful invasion of Cabul by the British—Whig policy opposed by the Tories—Army of the Indus—Importance to England of the Cabul conquest—Destitute condition of the British army—Signal failure of the expedition against Cabul—True policy of England in Cabul—Genius of the Avghan institutions—Abuses of the English policy in Cabul—English diplomacy at fault—Avghans fierce, semi-barbarous, and unconquerable—Intricate topography of Avghanistaun—M'Naghten's false policy—Cruelty of the English—Citizens of Cabul favourable to the English—Murder of the Russian ambassador in Persia—City of Cabul shelled by an English mortar battery—M'Naghten killed—Dismal prospect of the British army—Alternative—Indian troops contemptible—Proper military movement for the English—Metropolitan importance of Cabul—Ability of Cabul to provide for the subsistence of a garrison—Treasonable treaty of the English functionaries—Origin of the feud betwixt Shah Shujah and Dost Mahomed—Origin of Dost Mahomed's power—Origin of the war of the British with Dost Mahomed—Policy of Dost Mahomed—English diplomacy at fault—Consequences—Policy of Shujah—*On dit* of Russian policy - - 1

CHAPTER I.

REPLY TO COUNT BJÖRNSTJERNA'S WORK ON BRITISH INDIA—Preliminary remarks—Sources of information on India, Persia, and Avghanistaun—Value of the Count's opinions illustrated—His misstatements displayed and corrected—His false inferences from philology—His assertions false and inconsistent with himself—Historical fact misstated—Inquiry into the stability of the British tenure of India—Power of opinion—Routes into India—Proper route into India from the north of Europe—Topography of the routes into India—Population of British India—Diplomacy the weapon for Russia—Political obstacles to an invasion from the North removed—Russian Policy in Persia—Persian policy—Uzbeck policy—Russian influence in Central Asia—Inducements to invade India—Reflections on the progress of civilization—Missionary efforts in India—Traditionary prophecies of the Orientals—Eastern Question—American missionaries—Moral condition of the Asiatic—Russia preferred to England by the nations of India - - - 25

CHAPTER II.

REPLY TO COUNT BJORNSTJERNA'S INDIA, CONTINUED—Misrepresentations confuted—of topography—of moral obstacles—Avghan policy—Practicability of Avghanistaun for artillery—Relative powers of the camel, north and south of the Caucasus—Consequences of English errors in policy—military insignificance of the Indians generally—Plan of a Russian invasion—Character of the British government in India—Policy of the English, and of Alexander the Great, contrasted—Plan of Alexander's conquests—His philanthropy—Antiquities still prove the extent of civilization—Results of the English conquests—of their abuses—Origin of the British power in India—Their artifice and duplicity—Their rule of "divide et impera"—Confirmation of the East India Company's power - - - - - 55

CHAPTER III.

GEOGRAPHICAL BOUNDARIES OF BRITISH INDIA—Character of the population—of the soldier—Physical powers—Evils of Fiscal policy—Mendicity and misery - - - 70

CHAPTER IV.

FOREIGN RELATIONS OF BRITISH INDIA—River Indus the natural, moral, and political frontier of India—Avghanistaun not a part of India—Effect of Russian influence - 76

CHAPTER V.

ROUTES INTO INDIA—Base of action against India—Resources of the Uzbeck States—Facilities of water carriage to the progress of Russian civilization in Central Asia—Accessibility of India from the north—*Note*, Origin of the name "Peshour"—Greco-Bactrian dominion in Avghanistaun—of Parthian—*Note*, Cave of Prometheus—Persian dominion—Roman antiquities in the Panjab—Scythian dominion in Cabul—Toorkey—Princes of Ghoree—Modern Persian inroads—Ahmed Shah—Size of the English dominion—Importance of Bulkh as a military position - - - 80

CHAPTER VI.

REFERENCES FROM ENGLISH AUTHORITIES ON THE FOREIGN RELATIONS OF BRITISH INDIA—Ava—Nepaul—China—Internal discontent—Nepaul and Kandahar—Cabul—Russia—Heraut'h—Ava—Nepaul—Internal discontent—Russia—Agitation by the native Indian press—Persia and Russia—Domestic politics—Military weakness—Policy of Russia—Threatened dangers of the Indo-British Empire from foreign causes—Domestic dangers—Fear of Russia—Idem—Mysterious conspiracy in the south—Extract from the debate in the House of Commons on the motion for a vote of thanks to the army of the Indus—Importance to the English of the Cabul conquest - - - - - - - 94

CHAPTER VII.

Descriptive Character of Dost Mahomed—Birth—Parentage—Profession—Kills his brother's enemy—Military accomplishments—Habits—Early display of diplomatic tact—His policy—Rise to political power—Is a reformed drunkard—Literary pursuits—Becomes Ameer of Cabul—Relations with the Seiks—War with the Seiks—Retires to Cabul—Pursuits—Age—Personal appearance—Personal habits—Dress—Address—A politician—His eloquence—Timidity—Drunken revels—Anecdote of his rise to power—A reformer of morals—Questionable bravery—Despotic—His duplicity—Queen-Mother—His obstinacy and corruption—Licentiousness—Of the haram—His wives and children—His policy towards the English—His residence—Avghan plainness—His attendants and amusements—Routine of business—Ameer passionate—Secession of his brother—Military habits—Durbar—Ceremonies of Durbar—Meals—Cookery—Servants—Fruits—Pastimes and enjoyments—Evenings—Nights—Chess—Tastes of the Ameer—Fondness for story-telling—Allegory of Avghan avarice and poverty—His plainness—Military habits—His brother the Nawaub—His hypocrisy—His Veneration—Enthusiasm a religious principle—Motives of his political intrigues with foreign states—Seik

diplomacy—Ameer passionate—Secession of his brother—
Military habits—Attendants on the march—Daily routine—
Smoking—Domestic habit—Avghan civility—General drink
of the Avghans—Head of the Mahomedan religion—Ameer's
religious persuasion—Selfishness the key to his character—
—His financial abilities—Fiscal economy of the Orientals—
Origin of the Toorks—Their decline—Commercial commu-
nity—Ameer's rapacity—His mode of borrowing money—
Concluding remarks—*Note* diplomatic - - - 117

APPENDIX I.

ILLUSTRATION OF THE BRITISH POSITION AT JILLALABAD. 173

APPENDIX II.

ILLUSTRATION OF A TEXT FROM DANIEL, &c.—Eastern politics—England's unchristianlike position—*Note,* Eastern
Question—Fulfilment of prophecies—A point of Mahomedan
faith—Power of the sooltaun—His origin—Origin of his
power—His policy—Causes of the decline of Mahomedan
population—Source of revenue—Traditionary prophecies
current in the East—Allegory of Dijaul—Object of Christ's
advent—Remaining independent Mahomedan powers of
Asia—Christ the Soul of God—Volney's opinion of the dissolution of the Turkish empire—Mahomedans zealous for
the advent of Christ—Christians indifferent—Reproof—
Origin of the traditionary prophecies—Consequences of the
fall of Mahomedanism—Conflicting interests of the European
powers in relation to Turkey—Battle of Armageddon—
Restoration of the Jewish nation—Universal redemption—
Michael the Grand Duke of Russia to restore the Jews—
Warning and conclusion - - - - - - 178

APPENDIX III.

ENGLISH ACCOUNT OF THE MASSACRE - - - - 196

ERRATA.

Page 1, line 4th from bottom, for "later" read "late."
" 3, " " for "to whom" read "to those whom."
" 5, " 15th from top, dele "and."
" 12, " 16th " for "the" read "that."
" 16, " 13th " for "themselves" read "itself."
" 16, " 9th from bottom, dele "and."
" 21, " 8th " for "guerilla" read "guerrilla."
" 25, " 3d from top, for "Björstjerna" read "Björnstjerna."
" 26, " 12th from bottom, for "Björstjerna" read "Björnstjerna."
" 41, " 8th " for "Krauchee" read "Kranchee."
" 55, " 11th from top, for "Gujerath" read "Gujerat'h."
" 84, " 5th " note, for "Peukola" read "Pekhora."
" 85, " 2d " note, read "Finjan of Gholebund" is.
" 89, " 3d from bottom, for "Amir" read "Ameen."

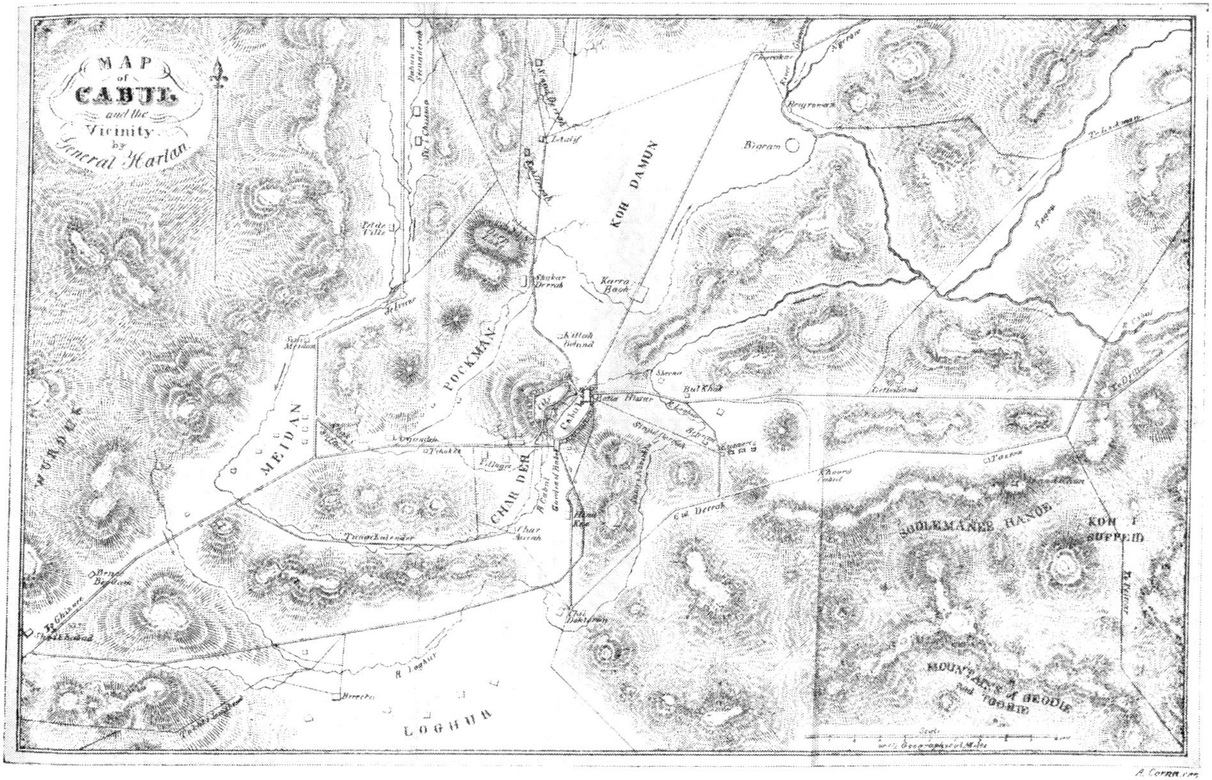
MAP
of
CABUL
and the
Vicinity
by
General Harlan
KOH DAMUN
POCKMAN
MEIDAN
CHAR DER
WURDUK
LOGHUR
SOOLEMANEE RANGE
KOH I SUFFEID
MOUNTAINS of BEODIE and TOORIE
Bigram
Cabul
A. Corna.

PREFACE.

The massacre *en masse* of a British army has awakened an intense desire for information concerning the people and the country which have been the cause and scene of that appalling tragedy, and produced in that feeling a result which the profoundest interests of philanthropy and politics, of religion and government, have heretofore, inauspiciously and unsuccessfully, strove in vain to accomplish.

From day to day our opinion is confirmed, and a long train of terrific disasters still mark the malignant track of that destructive meteor in the political history of England, " A Whig Ministry," as the frantic policy of British statesmen of that denomination *in India* astound the world with the developements of their awful and bloody sequences long subsequent to the origin of their designs.

Having been frequently interrogated concerning the probable consequences of the later movements in Avghanistaun, I think I shall not be intrusive by publishing, during this moment of general excitement, the ensuing pages, which were written in

January last, and are excerptions from my notes on "The British Empire in India." In thus anticipating myself I am guided by the wish to gratify public curiosity, and in the attempt to be explicit and comprehensive I trust my labours may not be found deficient in utility.

With the submissive resignation of a mind prepared to receive the decrees of incontestable destiny I recur to the maxim "The calamities of England are blessings to America"—and here let us deplore with the sanctity of filial piety the afflictions of our race. We breathe the requiem of our affiliated attachments, and say with the French, " Le roi est mort, vive le roi;" and as the *Te Deum* and *gloria in excelsis* mournfully ascend to heaven, let the voice float softly over the ashes of ten thousand dead.

Earl Auckland, Baron of Ghuznee,* and ye, innumerable host of subordinate moths whose "fire-

---

* Lord Auckland was created an Earl, and General Sir J. Keane was made Baron of Ghuznee; the first for planning the policy which, it was said, would confirm the integrity of the British Empire, and preserve India to England, by the conquest of Avghanistaun; and the other for the glorious campaign with the army of the Indus, that performed feats of valour rivalling the victories of Alexander, and exceeding the celebrity of his most illustrious adventures. Honours of knighthood, ribands, and brevets were showered upon the *conquerors* of the miserable Avghans with the unsparing liberality of royal munificence, which the breathless solicitude of imminent hazard wrought into existence.

new stamp of honour is scarce yet current," called into existence by the extinction of a free and, therefore, not ignoble nation, " will all the multitudinous seas" wash out the remembrance of your bloody deeds, or would ye, like Pilate, cleanse your hands after relinquishing your victims to the mercy of infuriated enemies. Englishmen, what says the award of conscience?

If the destruction of the British army involved no other consideration than the dreadful annihilation of so many wretched human beings, the soul would revolt from the view, and recoil within itself to avoid the contemplation of inhuman scenes so abhorrent to philanthropy. It is with feelings of profound regret that we mourn the departed; with unaffected sympathy we commiserate the afflicted and affiliated survivors of that fierce retributive visitation of Providence upon a sinning and incorrigible host; and as we implore the mercy of an offended Deity for the redemption of the *doomed*, we draw before our yearning faculties the veil of hopeless beneficence, trusting for all things in the mercy of heaven.

We turn now to the world, and with philosophy at our right hand, let us look at the balance which the inexorable " fiat justitia" has placed in the grasp of expediency, and behold the descent of power in the scale to whom hereditary right, and the force of circumstances, and command of position, all tend to establish and confirm a claim to supremacy. On this subject those who read the following sheets will readily form a just decision. Circumstances are displayed as they exist, and the power that Russia *could* exert, and the results, of tremendous import to the civilization of the human race, that must follow from the exercise of that power, are plain; but whether Russia has or will participate in the instigation of measures so prolific of benefit to man, the will of Providence alone can direct.

The English Tories believe that the Emperor Nicholas, like themselves, is and ever has been averse to the extension of dominion in the far East, which the principle of self-defence has heretofore forced upon these powers. " Whatever may have been the policy of Russian diplomacy," say they, " since the reign of Peter the Great, experience proves that the Emperor Nicholas not only avoids all cause of jealousy to England, but is even indifferent to the affairs of Central Asia."

The British in India are in the midst of danger without the interference of Russia. " God is great," but I cannot distinctly comprehend how the English, should they be forcibly dislodged, can either relinquish their hold on Avghanistaun with safety to their empire in the East, or recover their late position without incurring an expense of treasure and waste of blood which even the colossal resources of her government could not sustain. Their own experience in the American revolutionary war; that of the French in Switzerland; the Russians in

Circassia, and themselves again in Cabul, proves the utter folly of attempting to hold in subjection a hostile population. To conquer a dominion by controlling the political parties of a state is a feasible policy, or to reform by gradual means without annihilating the institutions of a subjugated country may be the effect of time and perseverance, but to subdue and crush the masses of a nation by military force, when all are unanimous in the determination to be free, is to attempt the imprisonment of a whole people: all such projects must be temporary and transient, and terminate in a catastrophe that force has ever to dread from the vigorous, ardent, concentrated vengeance of a nation outraged, oppressed, and insulted, and desperate with the blind fury of a determined and unanimous will.

Many are surprised at the apparent ease with which the English took possession of Cabul. This seeming phenomenon may be readily explained. The government of Cabul under Dost Mahomed was of an oligarchical form; he ruled as the paramount of many chiefs. When the British invaded Cabul, they were nominally led by Shah Shujah Ul Moolk, the representative of the ancient regime, who was to the Avghans what Louis XVIII. was to the French, but more popular than the Bourbon: he was surrounded by English officers, and sustained by a British army, who preceded all their movements by the alluring fascination of gold. Awakening the cupidity of the Cabul chiefs, they advanced to take possession, as resistance dissolved before the magic charm of Plutus, and each chief was literally purchased by coin and profuse promises to abandon the interests and fellowship of the ameer, and induced to embrace the *service* of the king. Nay, in their audacity they offered to purchase Dost Mahomed himself, by tending that prince a bribe to relinquish his sovereignty, and enter a prison prepared for himself and his adherents in the uncongenial climate of Hindostan!* The merits and demerits of the policy which suggested the invasion of Cabul, the march of the army, and their general mismanagement whilst there, have been much discussed. Their policy was opposed by the Duke of Wellington and the Tories, but this party, labouring under the curse of Whig measures, has been obliged to sustain the honour of the country and integrity of the empire, to carry out the mistaken and vicious views of their predecessors. They believe the *motives* of the Whig ministry were erroneous; that the pretext to remove the pestilence of Russian councils and intrigues from the frontier of India was founded in error, and that the object of the conquest, to con-

---

* The English proposed to the Ameer that he should accept a pension of £10,000 per annum, and retire into Hindostan. The prince, disdaining the ignominy of self-degradation, preferred exile, and he fled to Tartary. Subsequently he fought two unsuccessful battles with the English, and ultimately rendered himself a prisoner to the enemies of his dynasty. He was sent into India, and, I believe, allowed £20,000 per annum.

vert the country of an independent nation into a line of frontier defence, by occupying their strongholds as garrisons, and converting a whole nation into mere camp followers, was impossible and unnecessary; but now that the Indian government has involved itself in the responsibility of maintaining a paramount position in Cabul, to sustain her supremacy in India must continue firm in her designs, or relinquish the principle of her political existence in Asia. Great was the importance attached to the successful result of the invasion of Avghanistaun. An army of twenty thousand fighting men, accompanied by sixty thousand camp followers, thirty-five thousand camels, besides innumerable pack-horses and wheeled carriages for the transport of artillery, baggage, and commissariat stores, was concentrated in Scind, and leaving Sukkur Buckker as their base of action, penetrated with great waste of life and property, and expense of treasure, through the sterile, inhospitable, and desert wastes of Beloochistaun, debouching from the Bolan pass upon the plain of Quetta. The country consists of mountains divided by small unproductive valleys, with barely vegetation sufficient to sustain the pastoral population, which is sparse and savage. The quantity of water is only capable of sustaining small bodies of men and animals, and the army was necessarily divided into details to pass through a country where large masses must have perished from thirst. The camp followers were in a great measure unprotected, and subjected to the depredations of a hostile population: they were slaughtered in numbers; the baggage of the army was plundered by the predatory natives; their cavalry was exhausted from famine; their artillery horses, unfit to drag the guns, were led by the men; and they arrived at Quetta in a state of destitution little different from disorganization. Here a council of war was held, and the expediency of returning positively debated! The desertion of an Avghan chief* from the interests of the Kandhar Sirdars filled those leaders with the terror of domestic treason; panic fears pervaded themselves and their adherents, prompting them to sudden flight, and they became refugees at the court of T'heran. The British army advanced; Kandhar fell; Ghiznee followed; and the quiet occupation of Cabul ended an uncontested though expensive campaign, the operations of which originated causes of expenditure, against which the Duke of Wellington had prophetically forewarned his countrymen.

The fourth year is passing since the commencement of these military demonstrations: unheard-of obstacles have been subdued by dint of much human suffering; a king has been dethroned, and another restored; a kingdom lost, and won, and lost again. The Avghan people have been kept in commotion by continual domestic strife and civil wars; trea-

* Hadji Khan Kaker, created Nusseer ul Dowlah by the Shah —in reward of this treasonable desertion of the Kandhar chiefs.

sures exhausted; torrents of blood shed, and the whole affair terminated by the massacre of the invaders, whose numbers were said to be ten thousand souls. Thus the expedition has signally failed, and in that failure we behold the retributive justice of an avenging Deity; for those believe not in God who perform the deeds which characterize the misrule of England in the East; and they have received the punishment of Sennacherib for their infidelity, in the necessity of a just and merciful Deity, when English arrogance inconsistently proposed to supersede the order of Nature or the Divine Will, by enforcing the slavery of nations in the East, whilst engaged in the abolition of individual negro slavery in the West. Thus is England condemned by her own laws; and it is written, " out of the words of thy mouth shalt thou be judged."

The government of the Avghans by their own institutions would have been an experiment sufficiently facile, and a conquest, the achievement of which might have been effected with the pretext and the show of right. But no condition of submission short of absolute servility, and the abolition of their national identity, could satisfy the English in their projected conquest of Avghanistaun. They accordingly attacked the system of government, which has been the cherished form of society amongst the people from the earliest period of their political existence. The population is divided into numerous tribes independent of each other, every one separately governed by a chief selected from the oldest family in the community, though not always the oldest member of that family: the power is held during good behaviour, and in case of a vacany by death, an election is made of the heir of the late chief, or should he decline, a brother or near relation is elevated. The chief is to be viewed as an executive officer, and adminsters the laws of the tribe, which are the result of usage arising from expediency strictly in consonance with the customs of the people. He can levy no revenue; there are in fact no expenses of government. In a tribe each head of a family is a patriarch ruling in the undisturbed possession of his domestic hearth, bound by the common interest to sustain the peaceable and safe enjoyment of life and property of his community, and himself as an integral part thereof. The attachment of the people is to the community, and not to the chief, who is liable to be removed by a council of the tribe for any flagrant misconduct. The chief represents the tribe in their foreign relations, calls out and commands the militia, who maintain themselves, and administers the judicial system of his tribe. If the English had conciliated the heads of tribes, arranged them round the king, as sustainers of the government, which privilege they had a right to expect, they would have become willing hostages for the good conduct of their tribes. But the king, "who can do no wrong," drove these representatives of the people away from his court, seized and imprisoned many who presented themselves for employment and honours, telling them plainly his bayonets were preferable to their swords; deputed the offices of state to a swarm of hungry expectants, who attended him during his thirty years' exile, and filled up the appointments of revenue officers and governors of districts with household slaves and military retainers. These proceedings being sustained by the English gave rise to the prevalence of profound but subdued disgust, which lately displayed its effects in the sanguinary *finale* of the invaders. The English, who know well the value of gold, could have controlled the movements and policy of the Avghans by fiscal diplomacy, without incurring the odium of invading and subjugating an unoffending and distant free people, whom to subdue to European forms of civilization was impossible. They are but the " spirits of the waste" who inhabit the wild and sterile deserts of the Caucasian mountains. Their indomitable love of independence is characteristic and incorrigible. They are now what they appeared to be under the name of Bactrians in the muster-roll of nations as given by Herodotus in the expedition of Xerxes into Greece, the fiercest of the savage nations of Scythia. Kings have risen amongst the Avghans, and conquered India, but in retaining their conquests have relinquished their native country; they have been transiently subdued but never enslaved or permanently conquered and held in subjugation by a foreign power. The Greeks when they ruled Bactria, did so by a race of hereditary princes born in the country, who ceased to be subject to the Greeks in Europe. The experience of history, derived from the period of Alexander, from the legends of the Seleucidæ or the Greco-Bactrian successors to that dynasty, the invasion of the Parthian Prince Mithridates, or the defeat of Crassus, so similar in many of the incidents to the melancholy fate of " the army of the Indus," and the contemporaneous operations of Russia in the same range,—Cabul being on the eastern and Circassia the western extremity,—all go to prove the unconquerable nature of these semi-civilized communities inhabiting the vast range of mountains; and Lord Auckland, in place of being made an earl and receiving the thanks of Parliament and the Queen, should have been impeached, degraded, and despoiled of his hereditary honours.

I have appended a map of Cabul and the vicinity, by which the intricate nature of the country may be perceived by inspection. Sir William McNaghten was a self-conceited gentleman, who marched into Avghanistaun with the air of Bombastes Furioso, advocating to the governor-general a system of policy which has wrought the reward that cruelty, false faith, and criminal duplicity will ever receive. A nation whose principle of existence lies in the disunion and separate interests of its constituent tribes, became united by common oppression into one unanimous community, goaded to madness by the systematic and consecutive tyranny of their invaders. The populace were infuriated by a sanguinary and unjustifiable act, and in modern warfare, a measure of unheard-of barbarity, on the part of McNaghten. English papers of March 5th, state, "He requested the king to admit a mortar-battery into Balla Hissar, *to shell the town!*" to revenge the murder of Burnes, whose death was perpetrated by a body of religious fanatics, and not, as might be supposed from the bloody infliction of shelling a densely peopled city, by an insurrection of the inhabitants *en masse.*

The natives of the *city* of Cabul were the friends of the English; they had luxuriated several years on the fatness of English munificence, in the midst of an improvident soldiery,—wherefore was destruction rained upon them? If a public functionary had fallen in a popular commotion there, the recent example of the Emperor Nicholas in the case of Greybeadoff, his ambassador at the court of T'heran, who was murdered with all his staff in a popular tumult, might have suggested to Sir William the line of expediency; but those who disdain heaven, are vainly taught by the experience of man; and quick was the retribution of Providence for that black unnecessary deed of blood. When the mortar-battery opened on the city, and the confiding unoffending inhabitants, who had always been taught to repose on English justice, faith, and mercy, saw the mangled limbs of their wives, and children, and suckling infants, strewed about their domestic hearths, with a desperate and simultaneous impulse, they rushed on the commissariat godawns,* and another moment saw the British army in the grasp of an insulted and unrelenting foe. The headless trunk of their chief now lay weltering in its gory death—for McNaghten was murdered in a forced interview with the Avghans,—and they looked around in vain for the prospect of retreat. Their route for ninety miles lay through a mass of mountains, inaccessible at all seasons except by narrow defiles, in some places mere ravines or chasms in the immense alpine masses, often towering two thousand feet above the plain, from whose mural sides and elevated heights rocks and stones might be securely rolled down on the fugitives.

Now all nature reposed in her cold interminable sheet of snow. The inclemencies of winter, which always completely incapacitates the Indian soldier, were in their full prevalence in a climate where the earth is usually frozen hard as steel nearly four months of the year. They gazed upon the vast expanse before them; the mountains around them,

* Storehouses.

and all the country covered with snow, presented the dread result of a hopeless retreat; despair froze up the current of the blood as it curdled round the fainting heart; death stared them in the face with the option of starvation, of perishing through cold, or of dying with arms in their hands. Strange that a British army should not have chosen the latter alternative! If there ever was a doubt of the utter worthlessness of the Anglo-Indian army, on occasions of great emergency, and extreme peril, let this example suffice to set the question for ever at rest; for the English prints expressly state, as the cause of the massacre, that the Indian troops becoming disorganized, deserted their officers, disbanded and dispersed, some to safety and dishonour secured by treason, but many to death from the hands of an unmerciful enemy, or the still more merciless inclemency of climate. When the commissariat godawns were seized, the army of fighting men, which was just large enough to garrison the citadel called Balla Hissar, should have marched into that stronghold, which is entirely inaccessible to any mode of warfare of which the natives could avail themselves. They should have removed the population inhabiting the fortress, and they could have protected with their arms the inhabitants of the city, as it lies immediately under cover of the Balla Hissar, and they could have kept open a communication with the country through the citizens. There are several small forts and strongholds in various parts of the city; every large house has a strong portal and sort of bastion tenable against a siege if the assailants should be unprovided with artillery; each resident has a rifle, always ready for use, and the city of Cabul has, in fifteen minutes after the sounding of an alarm, been known to show upon the terraces of the houses, 10,000 armed men, fiercely bristling with the artillery of grim-visaged war. The city of Cabul has frequently rebelled against the king or its chief, during the civil wars of the ancient regime, and without extraneous preparation, readily sustained themselves in a s.ate of insurrection for thirty or forty days consecutively. During the winter, the citizens of Cabul have always six months' store of flour or wheat laid up in granary. The army might have been, by proper management, liberally sustained until spring; the English could have intrigued with the leaders of the opposing hordes, created conflicting interests amongst them, and formed a party by conciliation and diplomatic efforts, and dissolved a confederacy that threatened instant destruction; but the political affairs of the English had again fallen into the hands of still less competent agents: a young lieutenant of the Bombay Artillery, who is remarkable for obstinacy and stupidity, and an old invalid of high character and imbecile mind. All these facts may be easily proven, and the hands that signed the treaty by which a British army of 10,000 men has been betrayed to ignominious death, justly deserve the award of treason.

Thirty years have passed since the civil wars of Avghanistaun terminated for a brief period in the expulsion of the ancient regime. These wars were fomented, first by the pretenders to the throne springing from the common ancestor, Timur Shah, the progenitor and king who preceded the present incumbent, Shah Shujah. Causes of domestic conflict were kept in continual operation by the leaders of the Barikzye tribe, whose chief had been decapitated by order of Shah Zeman, the brother of Shah Shujah. The murder was avenged by the son of this victim of an evil policy, and this son, the Vizier Futty Khan, was the eldest of twenty-one brothers, amongst whom the Ex-Ameer Dost Mahomed is to be numbered. The worse than savage murder of Futty Khan by Kameran Mirza, son of Shah Mahmood, a successful opponent and half-brother of Zeman, whom he blinded, and Shujah, renewed the blood-feud betwixt the Suddoozye, or king's tribe, and the Barikzye, or tribe of the Ex-Ameer. The latter thoroughly and completely prevailed, under the direction of Mahomed Azeem Khan, the full brother and successor of Vizier Futty Khan; he was succeeded by his son Hubeeb Ullah Khan, who governed an insubordinate multitude, distracted with the vices of their princes, until a long night of anarchy was dispelled by the advent of Dost Mahomed, who was called by an almost unanimous voice of acclamation to assume the reins of power, which the feudal lords of Cabul were ready to strike from the rude grasp of a depraved and monstrous voluptuary, a young man, his nephew, eighteen years of age, the slave of every evil passion. Dost Mahomed attained the sovereignty of Cabul in 1824, and was hailed by the feudal chiefs as head of an oligarchy. This form of government continued, through the troubled movements of a restless people, with whom the prospect of peace is ever the pretext of tumult and strife, until 1839. This community of scorpions was ruled by Dost Mahomed with results that confirmed his character for diplomatic tact. With the means of attaining those results the politician has naught to do. There can be no doubt Christian morals and philanthropy would have been horrified at the violence, cruelty, and savage barbarity of a prince, whose title to supreme power was sanctioned by his abilities in the administration of a remedy or prophylactic measure against all the moral and political depravity of a community upon which Rhadamanthus would have gazed with fatuous and timorous dread! The strongest proof of Dost Mahomed's firmness, decision, pertinacity, and *finesse*, is to be seen in the fact of his having instantly relinquished the pursuits of an habitual drunkard on attaining sovereign power, together with the simultaneous and sincere repetition of his example by all his companions in licentiousness and arms.

In the winter of 1837–38, an individual arrived in Cabul from the camp of Mahomed Shah, who was engaged in the siege of Heraut'h. He represented himself as a Russian courier, who came, it is said, with a complimentary letter from the Emperor of Russia, addressed to Dost Mahomed. The chiefs of Kandhar (the Ameer's brothers), had already acceded to a Persian alliance, and the Ameer, apprehensive of being superseded in the patronage of the Persian Shah or the Russians, commenced hedging between the three agents then at Cabul, representing Persia, Russia, and England. To the English he held out two stipulations, which he made the *sine qua non* of a treaty offensive and defensive, and the establishment of a garrison of British troops in the citadel of Cabul. viz.: a payment of twenty lacs of rupees, (two hundred thousand pounds,) and that Runjeet'h Singh should be obliged to relinquish his pretensions to the natural territories of Avghanistaun within or west of the Indus. The utter and deplorable incapacity of the English agent originated a line of bewildering policy, commenced in the feebleness of a narrow mind, and finished with a deluge of misery and blood. Such indeed was the expedition to Moscow, of which this is a repetition on a small scale; though the consequences may be more important to the social condition of man than the great political convulsion alluded to.

The tenure of British India, and consequently the integrity of the British empire, is at this moment sustained by a single hair, and that so tensely drawn that the slightest adverse movement will certainly snap asunder the retaining power. The thousand native princes of India are regarding with intense anxiety and ardent hopes the movements of the British army before the Khyber pass, and the fate of General Sale at Djillalabad. Every able-bodied man, whose numbers are not less than *five millions*, covetous and exasperated enemies, is standing with " the foot in the stirrup and hand on the spear," gloating on the hope of plunder which the traditions of old age have placed in fascinating visions before them. The sentinels are in the watch-towers and their runners are in the way,—and the earliest promulgation of the last reverses of the British in Avghanistaun will signalize the destruction of every Englishman throughout the whole of India. If the Avghans slaughter the remnant of British troops under General Sale at Djillalabad, *and defeat the British army* in its projected attempt to force the Khyber defile, the British power in India expires instantly, without a doubt, as it will without a struggle—except the death-throes of their officers, as the native army strangle them in their beds. The Indians can more readily perform than the Avghans could conceive. Simultaneous movement, whether the effect of design or fortuitous occurrence, or the consequence of circumstance, will eventuate in the same conclusion. So far in this massacre of the British army nothing has been effected to disturb the Anglo-Indian government. But the clouds that have gathered in the Indian Caucasus, and scathed with their lightning the British army, have not ceased to thunder on the invading host. Should they rain destruction on the beleaguered forces at Djillalabad, an electric shock will rapidly pass through the chain of connexion that unites the Indo-British empire throughout, and important consequences must ensue beyond the control of England, which will seriously derange the supremacy of that race in India. The Avghans can submit to be defeated daily during the next six months; news will reach us of the repeated *decisive* victories of the British forces; but we, who are acquainted with the value of an English bulletin, know that the *repetition* of a *decisive* battle implies the continual necessity for defensive operations— and the Avghans will conduct a guerilla warfare, which exhausts by the pertinacity of incessant assault. The English admit that their position cannot be maintained against artillery. Should Djillalabad be a defensible position against native aggression, which certainly is not the case, even in English hands, where the disparity of the antagonists is measured by thousands against hundreds in favour of the assailants, a deficiency of provisions will oblige these brave men to yield, not to their enemies, but to the dismal alternative of—*death.* Sir Robert Sale and the *English* troops under his command, when no other choice remains but the stipulation of death or dishonour will unhesitatingly prefer the grave of honour in place of honour's grave. I incline to the belief that circumstances will again fight for the Avghans and destroy the remnant at Djillalabad, in which case the garrisons of Ghuznee and Kandhar must follow in the same train of events that involves the safety of their comrades.

The English will endeavour to avail themselves of Shujah ul Moolk's influence to regain their position. They say, with singular *naïvete,* " the king refused to accompany us in our retreat, and was immediately able to surround himself with three thousand followers in the Balla Hissar." The king never desired any greater favour of the English than a loan of money, with which he proposed to restore himself in his own way, by sustaining a party until he could ascend the throne. He is now upon the throne surrounded by a strong party, and his first wish is to rid himself of English tutelage. He will probably consummate his purpose; and the English, when they trust to Shujah, repose upon a broken reed, which will transpierce the hand of confiding faith.

Whilst I write, (May 7th,) the last accounts from England say, "On the authority of a Berlin correspondent, upon whose information, derived through letters from Moscow, great reliance is placed, the Times states, that the Shah of Persia has marched against Herat'h at the head of 60,000 men, and that Russia has furnished a subsidy of two million rubles in order to enable the Shah to make the movement." If this statement is founded on fact, the fatal spell begins to work.

Note.—In referring to English policy, I trust my English friends will distinctly draw the line of separation betwixt the system that elicits restrictions, and the country at large, and allow me the privilege of admiring those whose friendship I claim, without ranking me amongst the enemies of their household gods whom we mutually adore.

INDIA AND AVGHANISTAUN.

CHAPTER I.

REPLY TO COUNT BJÖRSTJERNA'S WORK ON BRITISH INDIA.

I AM not acquainted with any historical subject amongst modern incidents which has been more elaborately or more ably treated by writers of eminent pretensions than the British Empire in India, an important phenomenon in the political history of the human race, and justly entitled to a careful investigation. The patient and persevering application necessary to eliminate from an extensive and promiscuous mass the atoms of a fair synopsis, deserves our warm approbation; and the individual who devotes himself to the task with the motive of communicating information of a nature so full of interest as the general advancement of knowledge involved and displayed in the events of history, is entitled to, and shall receive, our grateful acknowledgements for the admirable design; but the errors of a work, whether accidental or premeditated, cannot be redeemed by the merit of the subject; and we are particular in referring to the blunders of the treatise under review, because an invincible name does more to substantiate error than a controverted attempt to confirm a false position; the effort producing a conflict which must result in the predominance of truth; whilst the silent and unimpeached influence of a name imperceptibly impresses its force upon a plastic receptacle, and insensibly corroborates the grossest mistakes.

On this subject the most efficient information can be derived in a form sufficiently condensed for the general reader, from Harpers' Family Library, entitled "History of British India," in three vols. 16mo. If to this publication is added "History of Persia, from the earliest ages to the present time," by James B. Frazer, Esq., complete in one vol., with a map and engravings; and the well arranged and minutely true account of Avghanistaun, by the Hon. Mount Stuart Elphinstone, a synopsis of Indian and Persian history becomes available, including all that a philosophical inquirer could desire. Amongst the collaborators upon British India one of the latest candidates for public approbation is "Lieut. General Count de Björstjerna," &c. &c., (of Stockholm,) formerly chief of the staff, and at present Envoy Extraordinary and Minister Plenipotentiary at the Court of Great Britain. The Count is an admirer of the English government, and his work, for that essential cause, is, in the opinion of our great Colossus of the world, "judicious and luminous, and will afford more complete information on the *British Empire in the East* than any work of the same extent in our own language." (Preface of the English translator.) The Count has laboriously referred to all accredited authorities on India, and enumerates more than one hundred published sources, besides a host of unpublished manuscripts, many of them voluminous deposits in the archives of the East India Company, from which his knowledge has been culled, and his opinions made up or confirmed. He presents himself to the public as an individual perfectly acquainted with his subject, and consequently soliciting and deserving the attention of his auditors, and doubtless, in default of more correct knowledge, he may bear away the compliment of merit which his pretensions in no kind justify us in awarding.

The Count is more than unfortunate in almost every opinion he has expressed. He is indeed unwise, for he compromises by his misstatements, in the fullest latitude, the gratuitous approbation of his English friends. The value of the Count's opinions and accuracy may be readily estimated at the onset by recurring to his puerile inferences drawn from facts which, in his imagination, are worthy of remark. He directs our attention to a wonderful coincidence, a discovery unthought of heretofore, and refers to the occurrence with a matter-of-course sort of self-complacency of an edifying caste. He says, p. 10 of "The British Empire in India"—" During his residence in India (1324-53) Batuta gained the favour of Mahomet, the Emperor of Delhi, who sent him on an embassy to the Emperor of China. Mahomet was *descended* from the Sooltauns of Khorassaun, who had conquered India. The *whole dynasty* of these sooltauns had the surname of *Oddin*, a circumstance which I consider it *right* to notice here." By referring to the History of India mentioned above, page 184, we see, " In the year 1316 the crown (of Delhi) was placed on the head of Mubarrick I., one of the Emperor's sons. He was murdered after a reign of three years, and amid the confusion which followed (p. 185), Tuglick, a *slave*, belonging to the warlike border tribe of the Jits, ascended the throne." Tuglick *was succeeded* by his son Jonah, who assumed the title of Mahomet III.; but instead of following his father's example, his crimes surpassed those of his most guilty predecessors, and made him, during a reign of twenty-seven years, the execration of the East. " Mahomet, it appears (p. 186), had at length resolved to adopt a milder system, but death interrupted him before he could realize his intentions, and delivered India from the dreadful scourge of his government in the year 1351."

This Mahomet was the son of a slave, and not, as the Count observes, " descended from the Sooltauns of Khorassaun," &c. " The whole dynasty of these sooltauns (those of Khorassaun, who had conquered India,) had the surname of Oddin." Merely alluding to the culpable and inexpressive looseness of the Count's style, we must meet this assertion with a direct denial. The first person who reigned as a local Mahomedan prince in India, was Kuttub ul Deen. He was of the humblest birth, having been purchased as a slave at Nishapoor in Toorkistaun. Mahmood of Ghoree established Kuttub as his lieutenant in the city of Delhi, on the subversion of the Hindoo dynasty. He was the first of a race of foreign rulers called the Patan dynasty, but his power did not descend in his own family. He was succeeded by Altumish, who, like his master, had been a slave. All the kings of what is called " the Patan dynasty," i. e., those who followed Kuttub ul

Deen, to the period of the Moghul dynasty, established by Baber in 1525, are mentioned in history by their proper appellatives, without a surname. It is probable some who were elevated from a low condition, may have had the surname of Ul Deen, according to the Mahomedan usage. This cognomen would have corresponded with the denomination of those who were called after some attribute of the faith, whilst there are many names which would not admit of the association. Such are Mahomed, Kei Kobad, Kera, (unless this last should be intended for Khire,) Ghuffoor, Omar, Mubarrick, Tuglick, Mahomed, *et id genus omne*. Admitting, for the Count's gratification, that they all took the surname which distinguished Kuttub, by what method of pronunciation, or by what value of letters, can Ul Deen be called Oddin. Ul is the Arabic article *the*, Deen means religion in the same language, and the word Kuttub signifies pole or axis (of the earth)— Kuttub ul Deen implies, "axis of the faith," i. e., the faith of Mahomed. The name is derived from the Mahomedan era, and cannot be in any way coincident with the Scandinavian name Oddin. Fancy the surprise of the Hyperborean worthy, could he break the cerements of his tomb at this moment, and find himself saluted by one antiquarian as a Hindoo devotee, whilst another familiarly addressed him as a Mahomedan priest! The Count's great discovery, of which he had so much to make in reserve, a circumstance which he sagely suggests, "I consider *right* to mention here," goes for naught.

The Count draws other inferences from what he considers coincidences of language, in each of which he still more strongly proves his ignorance of philology and of history, and deficiency in tact, in endeavouring to trace resemblances in sound without regard to orthography. In these results we can only lament the incapability of his views, and his frivolous pretensions, e. g.: fogdar, governor of a province, and fogdar, a word of the same signification in Sweden. Fogdar is pronounced in the Persian, fodjedar. It comes from fodje (*army*), and the imperative dar of the Persian infinitive dashten (to have), literally, the possessor of an army; colloquially, governor of a province. Again, Vedas, name of the sacred books of the Indians, is supposed to resemble Edda, by which name the sacred writings of the Scandinavians are known; also between Buddha and Oddin. Vedas is pronounced Bade, which is not a close resemblance to Edda, and Buddha becomes colloquially But'h, in the oriental dialects of Arabia, Persia, and Hindost'han, which in nowise bears any resemblance to Oddin, notwithstanding the Count's remarks, p. 63—" of these we may mention the resemblance between the names of Buddha and Oddin (especially in the oriental pronunciation)."

The foregoing are some of the " positive facts," which, according to the English translator, add an important zest to the Count's work; they show " the relation between the religious belief of the Hindoos and the worship of Oddin," (p. 10, Pref.) To show how little the Count has been understood by his English friends, if indeed he understands himself, let us refer to the remarks which he offers upon this subject, p. 65 et seq.: "Where do we find in the mythology of the Goths any traces of that love of allegory which so remarkably distinguishes the Brahminic doctrine?" &c. "No, the mythology brought by Sigge Fridulfson to Switheod had not its origin in India." " The doctrines of Brahma and Buddha are the products of India, originated on the banks of the Ganges, and *never* reached the shores of the Baltic." To make the worse appear the better cause, the Count even places his honour in an ambiguous and unenviable position. To what motive can we ascribe the relation of the following anecdote, intended as an illustration of the bravery of the Indian army? It is one of those unfortunate instances which prove more than the author intended or desired. The story is a prominent exception to the ordinary reputation of the Indian army, and shows that a circumscribed operation of an estimable quality is the result of a general deficiency. The conquest recorded is utterly false. Page 155: " As one among thousands of examples of bravery which distinguishes the soldier in the Anglo-Hindoo army, we may cite the following: In the year 1804, General Lake besieged the fortress of Bhurtpore, situated in the central part of India, which was considered impregnable. Holkar, after having lost two battles against General Lake, had thrown himself, with the remains of his Mahratta army, into the above-named fortress, and determined to defend it to the last extremity. Four attempts to carry it by storm had been repulsed, *the two last executed by the* 75th *regiment* of the English line, which had (like Ney) the surname of *les braves des braves.* A fifth attack was to be attempted. The *European* troops recoiled, when the 12th regiment of sepoys *offered* to undertake it, and planted their *victorious* colours on the high walls of Bhurtpore." Page 113, he says, on a previous occasion " Holkar was obliged to throw himself, with the rest of his army, into the strong fortress of Bhurtpore, which was besieged and stormed in vain four times, but on the fifth attempt *it was taken by General Lake!*" As national glory is a subject on which the English are peculiarly sensitive, we select the relation of the Bhurtpore affair, and the *singular* bravery recorded by the Count from their own annals: " Hitherto in general the reduction even of the strongest forts had proceeded in a sure and regular course; the trenches were opened, a storming party was selected, who forced their way in with greater or smaller loss, and were masters of the place. But the defenders of Bhurtpore not only fought with the most daring valour, but called into action means of defence and annoyance which the English had never elsewhere encountered, and for which they were wholly unprepared. They rendered the breach impracticable by raising behind it stockades and other bulwarks; they made the ditch unfordable by damming up the waters; and, during the assault, logs of wood, pots filled with combustibles, and burning cotton-bales steeped in oil were thrown down upon the soldiers. In short, the British army were repulsed in four successive attempts, sustaining in killed and wounded a loss of 3203, greater than had occurred in any two battles during this obstinately disputed campaign. *Even their glory was somewhat tarnished.* The seventy-sixth, (not the seventy-fifth,) *hitherto* the bravest of the brave, (*brave des braves*) and the foremost in every triumph, along with the seventy-fifth, (which here merely figures as an ordinary corps, and not the *brave des braves,*) *refused on one occasion to follow their officers* after the twelfth Bengal sepoys had planted the colours on the top of the rampart. Being bitterly reproached for having thus caused the failure of the assault, they were overpowered with shame, and entreated to be led to a last attack, where they displayed desperate but useless valour!

"It was now necessary to intermit the operations of the siege in order to repair the losses sustained, and to bring forward more adequate means of attack. The rajah, however, apprehensive of the final issue, and seeing that his entire downfall must follow the loss of his capital, made very advantageous overtures, including the payment of twenty lacs of rupees (2,000,000),* as the price of peace; while on the other hand the situation of affairs was such as induced the English general, on the 10th of April, to embrace the conditions, and even to promise, in case of a steady adherence to treaty, the restoration of the fortress of Deeg," (which had been taken a few days before.) Harper's Family Library, History of India, vol. ii. p. 169. I am enabled to add, that British policy induced the government to adhere to the treaty made by Lake in 1804; and that to 1825, when Bhurtpore was taken by Lord Combermere, the fortress had been a thorn in the apple of their eye. The natives for twenty years had boasted that the chief tower of their fort was built of the dead bones of their Feringee† enemies, cemented with the mortar of mud and English blood; that they had conquered the conquerors of India. Their pride and arrogance were inconceivably inflated; repeated insults had been inflicted on the English and their adherents; an Englishman could not pass through the district of Bhurtpore without great personal risk, and British officers on hunting excursions were

---

* £200,000.   † Frank, or European.

beaten and driven from the vicinity by the jealous natives with disgraceful impunity. The impression of its impregnability added audacity to insult, and to remove that conviction from the native mind, and ensure the moral subjugation of India, the conquest of Bhurtpore became absolutely necessary, and this result was accomplished by Lord Combermere, under the administration of Earl Amherst, in 1825.

After these preliminary strictures on the Count's "positive facts," I shall proceed to consider the 17th chapter of his book, entitled, "What prospect of stability has the British power in India?" The investigation of the British tenure of India is a delicate affair to the nervous excitability of the English upon this vital question. Involving as it does reasons forcibly bearing upon the integrity of the British empire, our great Colossus condescends to be grateful for a favourable opinion expressed by a foreigner, though in this instance no neutral. The Count cursorily, and with a tender admission of immunity, runs over the abuses of the English system, and after an unsuccessful attempt to exonerate his heroes, he philosophically concludes—"These answers to the reproaches which have been made to the British system of government and commerce in India, however plausible they may be, cannot wholly remove the grievances and their causes of fermentation in India, and therefore the British power in that country cannot be considered as properly consolidated," p. 202. He adds immediately, p. 203, "the question now is, whether the elements of stability overbalance the materials for fermentation existing in India. We consider the former to be the case, provided," &c. &c. Here the proviso includes principles of paramount consideration, and which would effect a great moral revolution, and thorough change, in the political and religious institutions of the Indian population, no less, 1st, than the just and wise government of the country; 2dly, the admission of the Indian people to a share in the government of the country.

The second stipulation is utterly opposed to the genius of the people, familiar as they are with the absolute form of government, which has existed amongst them for ages. The principle is incomprehensible to a community whose records, from the earliest period, enduring through thousands of years, show the devoted veneration of its masses for the patriarchal system. " Inspired," as the Count observes, p. 203, " with stoical and slavish indifference, which promotes obedience, and prevents the breaking out of insurrections against the existing power, and the belief in the transmigration of souls causes life to be considered as so insignificant a part of their eternal being, that it is not worth while to trouble themselves much about it." Much less, then, would they be likely to value highly a greater share in the government of their country. Again, p. 203: " It is often said, and I believe with truth, that the power of England over India is a power depending on opinion." Page 206: " In considering the stability of the government, or the result of a great military enterprise against India, we shall confine ourselves to the military (viz.: the strategetical, topographical, and statistical) part of the question, leaving the *political* as much as possible untouched." This is performing the play of Hamlet without the character of Hamlet. If the government is stabilitated on opinion or moral force, moral influence will be the proper weapon to oppose the government of opinion, on the accepted principle in war of man to man, and horse to horse opposed. But as the three points upon which the discussion of this momentous question is proposed cannot have the slightest bearing on the success of "a great military enterprise against India," I reserve my strictures on the Count's somnambulistic garrulity and general views, and on another occasion, by a simple statement of facts, I shall present the *political* part of the question, which the count, with much *naïveté*, professes to have a "wish to avoid."

On the subject of accessible roads into India, the Count is equally infelicitous. Having disposed of all the dangers from foreign invasion by shutting up the routes to India, he directs our attention to the passage across the Hindoo Kush as the road by which a Russian army might most easily penetrate to India. I have no doubt an offensive measure against India might be effected by this route; it is one of the accessible points, but not the most easy. Where the Count supposes the country to be covered by eternal snow, that is, the district between the Hindoo Kush route and Heraut, " over which there are no roads and where it is impossible for an army to penetrate," there passes a route via Bameean, diverging at Rooey, and debouching upon the plain of the Oxus, via Heibuck on the east, and Derrah i Esoff on the west, the first egressing by Tashkhoorghan (Khoolum), and the last between the cities of Bulkh and Mozar, which are respectively situated about six or seven coss* north from the mountain range. This is the great caravan route, and has been used from the earliest periods. It was by this *impracticable* route that Alexander marched from Bulkh,

---

* A coss is one mile and three-fourths.

(the ancient Bactra,)* and whose footsteps were retraced by successive invaders of India; of the Parthians under Mithridates, the Persians of Darius Hystaspes, and of Artaxerxes; of the Samanian, Toork, Moghul, and Persian dynasties. The Count commences at the beginning with a Russian invasion, and this is his first principle: " A Russian army intended for an expedition against India, starting from the eastern side of the Caspian Sea, and following the line of the Oxus, *must* be collected in Orenburgh," p. 220. This is true, but the result of the Khiva expedition proves that an attempt to penetrate through Khwarizm never should have been undertaken, and that a Russian army attempting to reach India *to be successful* should *not* start from Orenburgh. He is right in making Bulkh the working point, and in cantoning the Russian troops there. If he selects the route that has been travelled by all the great invaders, depredators, and conquerors who have infested India, he will get there with no less facility than a Russian army could march from Tilsit to Paris, over a macadamized road, and through a country yielding supplies in profusion.

I shall not follow the Count every step from Bulkh to Attock. The country is filled up with great mountain ranges, the routes are through narrow defiles, ravines, and upland valleys, and over passes rising sometimes to the gelid altitudes of perennial snow. They are difficult from the sterility of the soil, sparsely cultivated, the predatory habits of the people, whose pursuits are pastoral, their numbers few, and dispersed over an extensive surface. The Indian Caucasus, or that part which lies between Bulkh and Cabul, is three hundred miles broad, and the

* The city is called Bactra, and the province Bactria, by Q. Curtius.

highest pass is 12,500 feet above the sea. The roads are free from snow from May to October inclusive, except that by the Hindoo Kush, which is open from July to September inclusive. The route by Bameean is not subject to avalanches near the highway, as the Count infers, neither has a caravan ever been lost from any other cause than the predatory practices of the natives. The natural obstacles are by no means insuperable, for I have crossed the Paropamisus by this route commanding a division of the Cabul army, accompanied with a train of artillery, consisting of four six-pounders and two battering guns. They were dragged across the mountains on their carriages, and the whole distance was performed without the necessity of striking a pioneering instrument into the ground! I avoid following the Count from Bulkh to Attock, because a Russian army would never find the route contested; and physical difficulties, should they not be insurmountable obstacles, may be subdued by perseverance and enterprise. Should a Russian army ever take up a position at Bulkh, there will be an end to the empire of opinion in India; and there is not a stone or a stick in all the country which would not become a deadly weapon in the hands of outraged millions, to drive out the pitiful handful of European oppressors, amounting to some thirty thousand Englishmen, in a community which by the *Count's* showing is 200,000,000 (two hundred million) souls.* It is frivolous to dwell on the geo-

---

* The estimated population of India being represented by Björnstjerna at 200,000,000 is an error of 60,000,000; it probably proceeds from his ignorance of the geographical divisions of the Mogul Empire, within the boundaries of which, in its utmost extent, the amount of 200,000,000 has been stated. We can only account for this vast discrepancy by supposing that some districts have been twice computed, and thus swelled the gross

graphical difficulties and topographical impediments when they are not insurmountable obstacles in themestimate beyond the truth. The following statement is derived from *parliamentary reports*, which must be admitted final and unerring in a matter of statistics, when unequivocally represented in that light, viz., in the year 1832:

	Square miles.	Inhabitants.
Presidency of Bengal	220,312	69,710,071
Doubtful districts	85,700	
Madras	141,923½	13,508,525
Bombay	59,438¼	6,251,546
Doubtful districts	5,550	
	512,923¾	89,470,152

The population of the doubtful districts, being situated on the Nurbudda in Berar and Concan, is probably not large; so that the whole will not much exceed 90,000,000. The territory of the allied or protected, i. e., the subject states, is estimated at 614,610 square miles. Their population, however, is not supposed nearly equal to that of the territories under the immediate government of the Company. Mr. Hamilton, in the second edition of his Gazetteer, estimates it as follow, viz.:

The Nizam	10,000,000
The Nagpore Rajah	3,000,000
The King of Oude	3,000,000
The Guickwar	2,000,000
The Sattarah Rajah	1,500,000
The Mysore Rajah	3,000,000
Travancore and Cochin	1,000,000
Kotah Boondee of B'hopaul	1,500,000
Rajpootanah and other petty states	5,000,000
	40,000,000

The same gentleman makes the following conjecture as to the states that were independent in 1832, viz.:

Scindea	4,000,000
Lahore, Rajah Runjith Singh	3,000,000
Sinde	1,000,000
Nepaul	2,000,000
Cashmere and other districts belonging to the King of Cabul	1,000,000
	11,000,000

This would give a population of 140,000,000 souls for the whole of India.—*History of India*, vol. ii. p. 291.

selves, but derive their importance from political causes. They may serve for positions of defence to a hostile population against an invading force, but become the strongholds of friendly power when an advancing army can claim or command the sympathies of the people through whose territories they are to pass. Diplomacy is the weapon which Russia has to wield against the Indo-British empire, and by the process of diplomacy I shall show by and by that the British power in India—that empire of opinion which has so astonished the world by its unique existence,—may be made to disappear, and "like the baseless fabric of a vision, leave not a wreck behind." Page 223: "The road from *Peshour to Attock** goes through a narrow pass, formed by the Cabul river on one side and a high range of mountains on the other." It is difficult to imagine how the topography of a district should be so absolutely misrepresented as the Count's assertion here displays the face of the country from Peshour to Attock. The plain of Peshour is bounded on the north by the Cabul river, and on the south by a semicircular range of mountains in the district of Khuttuck. This alpine range commences at the Attock, and sweeps towards the S. and S. E. until they plunge into the Afreedee mountains of the Soolemanee range, behind or west of Peshour. The breadth of the plain included between the Cabul river and the southern boundary at its widest part,

---

* Elphinstone says, "On the march of the 18th, which reached to the Indus, the *hills* came close to the river of Cabul, so that we were obliged to cross them. They *belong* to the same range which we passed near Cohaut," &c. &c. They belong to the Khuttuck range, i. e., they are a lateral spur of hills springing from those mountains.

is thirty-five miles across, and nowhere do these mountains approach the *Cabul river* so as to form a defile. From Peshour to Attock the distance is an open plain, cut up into ravines as you approach the Attock; and still nearer this river there is a difficult pass over a spur of the Khuttuck range near the Cabul river, but it does not command the access to the Attock, except by this one road. The river Indus is accessible by several proximate routes. " There are *political* hindrances, which are of more consequence than the former" (geographical and physical). On this, to the Count, forbidden subject, viz., the *political* reasons affecting the stability of the Indian Empire (see p. 206), there seems to be no objection to avail himself if the argument makes against the enemies of England, which the Count supposes is the case here. But, as usual, he is again wrong when he ventures on an opinion, no less than he is false in the selection of his facts. He says, p. 223. et seq., "A military expedition from Russia to India presupposes that all the countries between them should first be subdued." Well, they have been subdued, but not by Russia. England herself has removed that obstacle to the advance of a Russian army by extending her frontier into Avghanistaun, and drawing a line of defence from the Indian Ocean at Kurauchee to Heraut, and thence through the Indian Caucasus east to Attock, so that there is no longer any neutral ground remaining between these two antagonist powers.

And is the Count so utterly ignorant of Russian influence in Persia as not to know that the interests of these two governments are intimately blended together, and identified with each other? That the

Shah of Persia is maintained upon his throne by the Russian power, in defiance of innumerable pretenders, claimants whose pretensions are by no means insignificant; and should their rights be left to the arbitrament of civil war, independent of foreign influence, would expeditiously dismember the Persian kingdom? That the monarch of Persia is swayed by the policy of Russia, and could at any moment conduct a Russian army from its point of concentration at Asterabad via Meshud and Meimunnah to Bulkh? It would not be more difficult to procure by treaty with the paramount lord of the Uzbeck states, the Ameer of Bocharah, a free passage and feudal service through his dominions, if necessary, to join issue with the proximate and mutual enemy at Cabul; the more especially as that enemy is a Christian power whose late conquests in Avghanistaun have brought to the threshold of Tatary the enterprising and heretofore invincible conquerors of the Moghul Empire. So long as England remained behind the Sutledge, and her views of aggrandizement were not disclosed by the late mighty stride into Central Asia, which brought within the circumference of her power the four independent principalities of Beloochistaun, Avghanistaun, Panjab, and Scind; the Uzbecks of Central Asia* might have justified a jealousy of the Russians, and also of the English, thinking themselves capable of maintaining their neutrality whilst the competitors for

---

* The Uzbecks of Central Asia, who constitute the only remaining independent Mahomedan communities, are: Province of Bulkh, Kundooz, Bocharah, Kokand, and Khiva the capital of Orgunge, or Khwarizm. These countries are bounded on the north by Orenburgh, east by Yarkand, west by the Caspian Sea, and south by the chain of the Indian Caucasus.

territory in Asia were equidistant, but the unexpected advent of a British army, the sudden conquest of Avghanistaun, and dreaded proximity of the English in the permanent occupation of Cabul, impresses a sense of terror and profound awe upon the only remaining independent Mahomedan communities of Asia, and drives those governments lying between Cabul and Orenburgh to solicit the approach of Russia as the sole antagonist capable of withstanding the tide of British conquests, which threatened, by the subjugation of Avghanistaun, to involve within the folds of her power the province of Bulkh, the principality of Kundooz, the Khanauts of Bocharah and Kokand, and the province of Khwarizm, (or Orgunge, of which Khiva is the capital.) These states are connected with the Russian empire, geographically, commercially, and by political identity, so that their interests on one hand, and their necessities and sympathies on the other, bind them to Russia in a manner inimical and hostile to the British government. Russia has thoroughly and firmly established a respect for her policy in Persia and the Tatar nations of Central Asia, including the Uzbecks of Toorkistaun, but not by conquest. Treaties offensive and defensive, and coveted guarantees of political supremacy to reigning powers, have been the means of subjecting expectant princes to the expanding policy of Russia, whilst the sword and bayonet have aggrandized by permanent occupation their less fastidious antagonists.

The Russians are viewed by the Mahomedans of Asia as a power whose civilization flows through the mild and fertilizing streams of commercial enterprise; whilst the English are viewed as the avaricious and bloody votaries of devastating invasions who recklessly sacrifice all that oppose their own love of independence as a bar to their ambitious projects. The Russians, far from being obliged to conquer every petty state between Orenburgh and Attock, would, upon the mere suggestion of an Indian invasion, have the hordes of Central Asia clustered under her patronage, nations of feudatories, propelling in her train their armed hosts, dense clouds of cavalry thundering at her heels over the waste and unprotected plains of "the Indian paradise, where the stones are gold and jewels, and the dust of the earth ambergris and musk." The prospect of plunder to the feudal masses of India and Central Asia, the chances of aggrandizement held out to native princes from the breaking up of an immense empire, the spoil of cities and of usurers, whose coffers are annually replenished with six-tenths the gross revenue of India,* were strong inducements, if incitement were necessary, to the hungry maw of native cupidity, restrained in tiresome monotony and endurance of a grinding and exclusive system of European rights, engrafted by the English upon the free, the reckless, the untrammelled, though absolute legitimacy, of the feudal order of society as it exists in Asia. Civilized man is the creature of habit; the semi-barbarian is more the child of nature: both are modified by education. The education and moral regimen of Asia is purely oriental, whilst that of Europe is no less local and adapted to the demands of European wants. The West and the East are diametrical antipodes, each possessing principles, systems, and morals *sui generis* and respectively characteristic of

---

* The gross revenue of British India is £21,000,000 sterling annually.

each. No amalgamation has been effected. As they were during the Crusades they still remain. There is no sympathy between Hindoo, Mahomedan, and Christian communities; all are at variance, antagonist, hostile, and unrelenting enemies. Masses of population thus disposed will not be refined by promiscuous intercourse. Each one confident in his own philanthropy would confer the beneficence of his peculiar institutions on the other, and so long as the struggle of their respective systems is confined to moral influence, 'tis easy to foresee the inutility of the result. Christianity is truth, and truth, however sustained, is justified by the means. The sword may establish the truth; the pretext and the impositions of vice it needs not. These are dimming clouds that obscure the soft rays of mild religion, and present her to the world like the blessed sun shorn of his beams, a sanguinary emblem of threatening futurity. When the Sun of Christ rose upon the throne of Constantine, the sword of state cut off the Pagan gods of infidel Rome. Masses of population, constituting millions of souls, with identical prejudices, feelings, and passions, are operated upon *slowly* by the imperceptible influence of mind, as it becomes developed by the stimulating necessities of observing man. Experience is the great, the practical teacher of mankind, and the founder of progressive civilization. Education but serves to elucidate the medium, and render experience available. The moral instruction of Asia originates in experience, and expands over the surface of society as it is solicited by necessity. Our book-learning of the West, which is the drapery of our civilization, and springs from a previous acquisition of taste for the beaux arts, is unknown and unappreciated by the Asiatics, rudely occupied as they are in hourly, in painful industry, in momentary and anxious solicitude for their daily rations; the ease, the leisure, and the luxury of wealth they know not: these are the privileges and acquirements of the divine and absolute few whose artificial powers of government enable them to subjugate the minds of men! Nothing has been done by missionary efforts or government institutions towards implanting the love of knowledge or knowledge of learning among the masses of Asia. The tastes of the Orientals and their necessities are native to themselves and their soil, and different from European ideas; and all the pretended and ostentatious efforts of public institutions, the munificence of private enterprise, the vain show of government designs, politically insincere, and the austere devotion of holy missionaries, are local and circumscribed, confined to occasional and solitary cases, or utterly insignificant results; such as attend the benevolent and pious complacency of European Roman Catholics, who despatch the self-denying disciples of their faith commissioned to implant their creed amongst the schismatic millions of America. Except in the chief cities of India, and those more immediately under European control, such as Calcutta, Benares and Delhi, Madras and Bombay, and the military cantonments of the English, the native community knows nothing of European institutions. The masses of Asia, stupified by ignorance, apathetic from climate and physical imbecility, are at the bottom of the social order. To move them by education a lever would be required which twenty millions of teachers could not do more than render effectual for instant and general utility. " Of the one thousand millions of inhabitants (says the Count) upon the globe's surface, we have three hundred and eighty millions of Budhists, two hundred millions of Hindoos, one hundred and forty millions of Mahomedans," besides millions of Jews, Guebres, and infidels amongst *nominal* Christians, all inhabiting Asia—a magnificent and unbounded field for missionary efforts, at which hope would sicken and the heart fail, were we not assured that "the Lord shall pour out his spirit upon all flesh, and every living thing shall be taught to know God." To that miracle we should trust for the consecration of our confidence in heaven, whilst we bless and admire the universal and devoted enthusiasm of those self-denying disciples of Christianity who plunge into the fathomless sea of barbarism in search of an oasis of Divine love, where the little grain of faith may be sown for the salvation of future generations,—or boldly stalk through the fire of probation, unscathed by the seven times heated furnace of infidelity, as they strive against the ignorance and apathy of man that *will* not be blessed.

It has been observed by historical authorities, "The results produced by missions under the different societies in various parts of India, is extremely similar. The natives have every where become *secure* from the apprehension of any violent attempt to overturn their religious belief and observances. This confidence, instead of being shaken, seems *confirmed by the presence and activity of the missionaries;* when they see the *government* at the same time *maintaining the strictest neutrality*. They have even overcome all fear arising from the intercourse of foreigners with themselves or their families. They are fond of meeting and entering into argument with them, which fact implies contempt of the missionaries' abilities; they send their children to their schools from motives of worldly consideration, that they may become qualified as subordinate clerks in the commercial establishments and government offices, and even allow them to be catechized and instructed in the doctrines of Christianity; though there is a conservative society of the Hindoos in Calcutta, which has a newspaper published under its patronage, who excommunicate from their community every one who is known to countenance innovations upon their ancient established systems of religion and education, or the ordinary habits and customs; yet with this, the examples of conversion are so extremely few, that, in a *national* sense, they may be considered *as nothing*. Omitting all consideration of the manner in which the Hindoo religion is interwoven with the habits of life, with the splendour of its festivals, and the zeal of its votaries, the single institution of Caste opposes a most formidable obstacle, though one which is sensibly diminishing through the continued communication of the English, and particularly of the missionaries; (this remark is at variance with the above mentioned conclusion, that all previous efforts go for nothing.) The circumstance too, that every particular of their creed and worship is in voluminous writings, all believed to be of Divine origin, renders it almost impossible to make *any* impression. However unable they may be to defend any of their dogmas, the simple remark, at the close of the conference, that 'it is in the Shastras or Vedas,' banishes every impression of doubt; they imagine that they can with perfect safety amuse themselves with disputation, and send their children to the schools with a view to their improvement or worldly advantage; nor do they scruple to appear in the character of what is called inquirers, and amuse their instructors with *deceptive* hopes of their embracing Christianity."*

The time was when twelve poor fishermen, destitute of moral influence or political power, were deemed by the Founder of our religion, a sufficient complement to preach the gospel to all mankind. One of the ablest and most eloquent writers, but the insidious advocate of infidelity, has laboured with sophistical arguments of well-drawn inference to prove that Christianity owed its progress to natural, and not to miraculous causes. Small and apparently insignificant in the commencement were the efforts which have issued in the mighty results of Christian conversion in the Roman world; and if natural causes, arising from so simple and unpretending an origin, were sufficient to supplant idolatry and establish upon the altars of "the unknown God" a communion of churches, comprising at this day 200,000,000 worshippers, is there not greatly more reason to indulge the hope of regeneration for Asia, although strong in her bulwarks of superstition, and apparently invincible in the possession of institutions venerable from their antiquity, and firm in their connexion with the prejudices of the people whom they concern? Previous to the conversion of Con-

---

* The Societies in Great Britain for the Propagation of the Gospel in Foreign Parts, are that of the Baptist persuasion, which commenced its efforts in 1792; the London Missionary Society, founded on a great scale, in 1795; the Church Missionary Society, instituted in 1800, which began its operations in India in 1812; and the Scottish Missionary Society, recently established at Bombay.

stantine, the fathers of the church did little more
than fertilize by their zeal the field of their labours.
The natural effect of new religions upon antecedent
systems of worship, when powerless and unsustained by political impulse, and after the bigotry of
persecution has become exhausted, is to create a feeling of indifference where oppression once prevailed;
carelessness begets impartiality; from long threatening, unattended by apprehended consequences, the
mind relapses into apathy, and the watchfulness of
jealousy is eluded. The institutions of a community
are never more liable to subversion than when the
prospect of innovation is regarded with familiarity;
the attempts of the charmer are crowned with
success when the object of his desires listens to his
voice; and the very confidence with which the
Hindoos are now inspired on the subject of conversion, shows they have been brought seriously to
contemplate the possibility of change. The missionaries are probably in the way of commencing
in Asia the epoch alluded to in the Apocalypse,
chap. xiv. 6., " And I saw another angel fly in the
midst of heaven, (*i. e.*, a space beyond the Roman
world,) having the everlasting gospel to preach unto
them that dwell on the earth, and to every nation,
and kindred, and tongue, and people." The missionaries perform their duty in *preaching* the gospel,
and the convert owes his regeneration to the spirit
of God. Coming events cast their shadows before,
and like causes produce similar effects. The incident succeeding John's vision is to be a great
political revolution; an event forming so important
an era that it alone is pre-eminently entrusted to
the promulgation of an angel, verse 8th: " And
there followed another angel, saying, Babylon is

fallen, is fallen, that great city," &c. The prediction indicates the overthrow of infidelity, prefigured by " Babylon," by the destruction of civic institutions; and without any other *miracle* than a Christian emperor's ascendant, we may see the altars of Paganism cast down, the prejudices of superstition rooted up, the bigotry and zeal of miscreant votaries swept away by the arm of political power, the edifices of idolatry reconstructed for Christian uses; and when the Crescent shall have been supplanted by the Cross, the " angel rising in the east,"*—whose commission is to stay judgment until the reorganization of the Jewish nation or twelve tribes shall have been accomplished,—finishing his charge, leaves the world free to the tramp of Russian hosts, we may behold established the cause of Christ in the East, and Nicholas become to our modern age the champion of principles, in advocating which the first Christian emperor immortalized the name of *Constantine*. Throughout all Asia, in every community and nation, Mahomedan or Pagan, there exist traditionary prophecies that a people whose significant characteristics designate the European race, is predestined to conquer their possessions, to subjugate their power, and establish a new order of government and religion; and the votary of Bramah, the disciples of Mahomed, the followers of Buddha, or the scholars of Fo and

* The Eastern questions in the politics of these days, that is, the diplomatic relations of Europe with the East, as evidenced in the conspicuous position of the five great powers of Europe in reference to Turkey, Syria, Egypt, Arabia, Persia, Bocharah, Avghanistaun, India, and China, in all which countries, England and Russia (the two ruling powers in the world) have especial political agents, actively employed in countervailing each other's influence, and establishing their respective interests.

Confucius, silently behold in solemn reverence the gradual approach of a great moral revolution, which the contemplative mind of their philosophy views with the unimpassioned and submissive resignation of fatalism. The science of astrology, so vaguely prophetic in its general sense in reference to the futurity of these nations, with wonderful congruity and unanimity of design conspicuously and precisely accords " the doom of unavoided destiny" a period not far removed into the uncertain shade of approaching time—implies the proximity of an event of which existing circumstances also denote the near completion.

The American missionaries are coequal in activity, in ability and disposition of talent with their European coadjutors, and whilst their pursuits are honoured and their motives revered by all interested in the evangelization of infidel or heathen communities, their singleness of design, confined alone to this imposing object, without in any way compromising their religious character with secular views, has frequently received the kind countenance and secured the gratuitous praises of officers high in the government services; their commendations attest the qualifications, the morality and the zealous devotion of our countrymen in the missionary cause. The American Board of Foreign Missions has established stations in numerous positions of Northern India, and their missionaries have proved themselves exemplary and honoured agents in a righteous cause. They have originated schools for the instruction of the natives in Christian literature. By the acquisition of the English language, which is taught through the medium of moral and religious books, the pupils are unconsciously led to embrace enlightened views of our civilization and peculiar institutions. The soil is fertilized, the seed is cast, and we trust in the mercy of heaven for the beneficent results. The American Board of Foreign Missions has established a typographical and lithographic press at Loodianah, conducted by their own agent and devoted to the publication of works useful in the dissemination of pious knowledge. Many excellent translations of tracts and parts of Scripture, selected by the judgment of men well acquainted with the moral wants of the people subject to their influence, have already emanated from this source. By the existence of this press upon the Seik frontier, a desire to examine the sources of European knowledge was generated in the mind of Runjeet'h Singh. A commission was appointed by that prince to investigate the facilities for getting up a printing press at his capital of Lahore. But these unexpanded hopes of progressive improvement in the Panjab have been blasted by the death of Runjeet'h, the removal of his dynasty, and consequent anarchy of the Panjab government.

The feudatory of Asia is still the child of nature, who disdains the restraints of civilization. With his horse in gay trappings of silver and gold, with his trusty spear in his hand, a sabre by his side and shield thrown over his back, he loves to prowl "*en cavalier*" upon his native deserts of plain and mountain, in pursuit of the chase or conflict of battle; and he covets the excitement, regardless whether the game be man or beast. A sharp sword and a bold heart supplant the laws of hereditary descent, and the physical powers of barbarous man supersede the quirks and quiddities of monotonous laws. The attempt of aspiring genius or audacious ambition gains by the sabre's sweep and soul-propelling spur, a local habitation in a kingdom and a name amongst the crowned subdeities of the diademed earth. In British India, the fascinating train of military glory, which is the soul-sustaining *spirituel* of feudal life, has been cut off by the matter-of-fact drill master. Under English domination we have his stiff encumbered gait, in place of the reckless impetuosity of the predatory hero. The cane of the martinet displaces the warrior's spear, and the formal close-set regimentals uncouthly usurp the place of the graceful flowing robes of oriental voluptuousness.

By the conflicting interests of Russia and England in Central Asia, the masses of India have been awakened to the antagonizing principles which divide the European nations. They are familiar with the struggle of democratic licentiousness against exclusive legitimacy; of divine right and representative privilege; of absolutism, and the rights of man. To them the English are the advocates of political infidelity, whilst Russia is the patron of conservative principles, the head of the feudal system, the sympathizing sustainer of sympathetic institutions. To Russia they turn as to their political Kibla, even as their myriads address their prayers in worship before the temple of Mecca, or adore the benignant face of the day-illuming orb. To Russia, with intense desire, the expectant people daily and hourly look as the power representing to them the Deity on earth; a saviour and protector; the restorer of their political rights, the dignity of their kings, the bygone days of glory for the soldier, of peace and plenty for the peasant; security, power, and wealth, with absolute sway to princes.

CHAPTER II.

REPLY TO COUNT BJÖRNSTJERNA'S INDIA, CONTINUED.

To proceed with the Count's work. Enough has been said to show that his enumeration of physical obstacles are for the most part imaginary, and his topographical " facts," almost without an exception, either false or exaggerated. He further remarks, "the Panjab is a marshy country, intersected by five great rivers," and I reply, that there is not a natural marsh in the whole country so large as the palm of my hand. A portion of the great Indian desert penetrates into the Panjab, and terminates in the province of Gujerath, near the Himaleh mountains, occupying the country between the river Hydaspes and Hydraotes, (the Jelum and Ravee.) Beyond this, extending to the Indus, are the sterile, argillaceous, and intractable upland plains of Potewar; to the south are the desolate tracts of immense jungle, consisting of high grass, dwarf bair, tamarisk, and baubul, so that the only productive and highly cultivated districts lie east of the Hydraotes, towards the Sutledge, and these are never marshy or even saturated, except during the rainy season, when occasional heavy falls of water effect a temporary lodgement upon the flat surface of a plain many miles in length and breadth, from the river Bias (or Hyphasis) to the Sutledge (Sudless or *Hysudrus*). Between these two rivers the soil is a fat vegetable mould, and the level of water is about three feet below the surface. Wells of this depth are sufficient for the purposes of irrigation, but the Panjab is *nowhere* marshy.* As for the rivers of the Panjab, I have crossed them all on horseback in the fall months; and during winter the Indus may also be forded on horseback, near to and above the Attock ferry, without swimming the animal.

The Count predetermines that Persia conjoined with Russia shall make no allies in a projected invasion of India. He alludes to the religious enmity existing between the Avghans and Persians: the former being orthodox Soonee Mahomedans, whilst the latter are the schismatic followers of Ali, known by the sectarian appellation of Sheah. I can inform the Count that the religious watchword of "Dum i char Yar" no longer calls together the bigoted Soonee to oppose the less infatuated Sheahs in their alleged desecration of orthodoxy; and that these disciples of "Shah i Merdan" were tolerated and caressed in Cabul under the strictly impartial government of Dost Mahomed. There is no doubt of the violent enmity mutually prevailing between these two denominations, but governments are ruled by expediency and not by religious bigotry or exasperated

---

* Kanawan is the name of a fen made by the expansion of a stream forming a tributary amongst the head waters of the Bias. It skirts the Himaleh range, northeast of Lahore, on the frontier of Nadoun, a principal town of the Katouch principality, not within the geographical boundaries of the Panjab, although it has been subdued and added to the political compact of the Seiks.

sectarianism, though passion influences a casting vote where policy does not oppose its voice. If the Avghans under Dost Mahomed saw that Russia and Persia united were *stronger* than England, they would have joined the former; if they suspected the allies of inability to withstand their enemies, they would have rendered their cause less hopeful by coalescing with their enemies. But now the English, having advanced into Avghanistaun and *attempted* the subjugation of their country, there is no longer a doubt but they would readily unite with the forces of Russia and Persia to regain their national independence; and the British, in case of an invasion of India by these powers, would be obliged to defend possession of Avghanistaun against a hostile population and a foreign enemy, and at the same moment to maintain their power against the fermenting millions in her Indian dominions, which position would be final and fatal. Page 227: " In these extensive sandy deserts which lie on the road to India, it is impossible for horses to draw the heavy artillery and its ammunition"—a gratuitous assertion, which any native of Avghanistaun, Beloochistaun, Scind, or almost any part of *Asia*,—except the great desert of Kobi, with which I am unacquainted, but upon which the Russian archives would probably enlighten him,—can tell the Count is not the fact. No native army moves without artillery. Dost Mahomed had sixty pieces of cannon, many of them heavy battering guns, drawn by oxen, and many pieces of horse artillery. Shah Shujah ul Moolk, in his military demonstration against Kaudhar in 1833, from Shaokarpore, had sixteen pieces of horse artillery collected between Loodianah and Scind; and the British army (1839), consisting of 20,000 fighting men and

60,000 camp followers, was accompanied by a regular train of artillery, consisting of heavy mortars, breaching ordnance, and light batteries, all of which were transported on their carriages by bullocks, by horses, or by manual labour. The whole country, from Meshud to Attock, where the open plains commence towards India, and from the river Oxus to the Indian ocean, has been traversed again and again by native armies, cavalry and infantry, caravans, and camels, time out of mind, with untrammelled facility, as appears from history ancient and modern, —from the days of Xerxes, "who stirred up all against the realm of Grecia,"* to the frivolous ephemera which emanated from the superficial military book-makers who accompanied the late English expedition into Cabul. Page 238: "Coming in the Avghan mountain passes, with their hard and stony paths, the camel is useless." Accompanying the English army from Shaokarpore via Kandhar to Cabul, there were thirty-five thousand camels, according to the verbal report of the fiscal agent at Cabul; many of these animals, bred in the plains of Hindostan, died from privation, fatigue, and climate; but seasoned camels, prepared to sustain these disqualifying incidents, native to Khorassaun and Tatary, are readily procurable for an army advancing from Bulkh. The Bactrian camels are the hardiest of all, and the Bughtee or short-legged animal, bred from the double-hunched Bactrian male camel, and the single-humped dromedary, is the strongest of its species, and capable of unexampled endurance. By the construction of its foot, which is provided with

---

* See the account by Herodotus of the muster-roll of Xerxes' army.

a longer toe-nail than ordinary to the dromedary, it is enabled to travel amongst mountains with ease. I have purchased this breed in Bactria, and found them excellent carriage cattle for crossing the Indian Caucasus. I escorted a caravan into Bulkh, or rather a caravan was allowed to accompany my division, when proceeding in the campaign against Kundooz in 1838-39. It was made up of 1600 camels and 600 pack-horses. We crossed the Paropamisus, via Bameean, Rooey, and Derrah i Esoff, debouching upon Mozar. The camel is the ordinary beast of burden in Avghanistaun. Travelling merchants or Lohanees pass from Lucknow in the heart of India proper, to Bocharah, the great capital of Central Asia, with at least 10,000 camels in their annual professional and migratory visits between these two celebrated marts of Oriental commerce.

The Count lays great stress on the physical and political obstacles to a Russian invasion of India, as they existed previous to the late conquest by England in Central Asia. All those difficulties refer to the topography of the country and government of the principalities lying between the frontiers of Persia and India. How much then does Russia now owe to England for removing all those safeguards to India, by advancing her frontier to Heraut, at once annihilating the neutral ground between her own empire and her antagonist, so that when a Russian army shall reach Bulkh, which is sufficiently accessible, they will forthwith come into conflict with the English at Cabul? Avghanistaun and Lahore, no longer allies, in which character the Count fancied a host of invincible friends, but with all the warlike and partially subdued communities lately* added to their troubled dominion, now decidedly exasperated into the condition of fierce and vindictive enemies, devoted to the revenge of their lost nationality, and ready to make common cause with the conquered princes of India proper.

Page 243: " A small army (inferring that a great one could not reach the Attock) cannot effect any thing on its arrival at the Indus against the superior British force there stationed, which, amply supplied with the necessaries of war, can compete, as well in discipline and skill, as in bravery, with any army in the world." Without entering upon the questionable merits of the Anglo-Indian army, I will merely observe, that the same resources are available to Russia as have contributed for England the means of the Indian conquests, and that the " skill and bravery" of the Indian population is nowhere more plainly demonstrated than by the fact that some 30,000 Englishmen have subdued 140,000,000 of them.

Again, if the Anglo-Indian army " can compete, as well in discipline and skill, as in bravery, *with any army in the world*," those same 30,000 English will stand a miserable chance of salvation against the Anglo-Indian army itself when sustained by 100,000 regular troops of Russia, and the myriads that will rally under her standard in an Indian expedition. The conquest of India by Russia involves an European question which will be decided when Constantinople shall no longer have a Moslem master; and this is a consummation which the fast

---

* In the campaign against Cabul, for the establishment of the ancient regime under Shah Shujah ul Moolk, in 1838-39.

progressing dissolution of the Ottoman power will quickly determine.

We conclude with the Count (p. 243) that "British India seems to have nothing to fear from an invasion by foreign armies, so long at least as tranquillity can be maintained in the interior of the empire." But internal convulsion is the necessary consequence of an invasion, and "the way to produce such a convulsion within the bosom of the empire in India would be, either to conquer by degrees (*subdue by treaties!*) one after another those states which lie on the route; to spread and exaggerate the reports of such conquests, and to excite those causes of fermentation already existing there; or, *what would be easier*, merely to *stimulate by political influence* the hostile sentiments of those states towards British India (*and of the Indian princes against the English*); to influence the desire which they have cherished for centuries to make conquests in that country; to organize their forces in the European manner, and, when the time is come, to give military leaders to their armies, and direct their strategical operations against India."

It is a mortifying conclusion, and an opinion no less true than humiliating, " that the measures of the Indian government *ought* to have more the character of stability than of movement, be suited more to the ideas of an oriental population than to those of an occidental. The first will quiet the millions of India, the second will frighten them as interfering with their *mental repose*." It is this principle which *does* control the British government in the administration of Indian affairs, and there is therefore *no movement* in any of the measures designed for India. Justly may we exclaim with Burke, that " the British empire in India is an awful thing." Whether viewed in regard to its responsibilities or its results it is indeed terrible and extraordinary. The government of 140,000,000 human beings, emphatically subject to the people of England and not to the crown, involves the British nation individually and collectively in the accountability of at least the system if not the administration of Indian polity. The conquests of Alexander were legitimated by the results of his victories. His power was extended by the sword and maintained by the arts of civilization. The savage Bactrians, the voluptuous Persians, the philosophical gymnosophist, successively submitted to his sway and received the civilization of Greece. Cities peopled by his camp followers and superannuated soldiers became the basis of his support in distant countries,* so that the Macedonian invasion was rather a migration of military colonies established throughout the wide-spread conquests of their leader, and remained a blessing to succeeding generations by the introduction of the refinements of life, the arts and sciences, in the midst of communities exhausted by luxury or still rude in the practices of barbarism—elevating these two conditions to the medium of nervous energy which characterized their invaders; yet the conquests of Alexander were effected by violence and haste, and

* There was an Alexandria founded near Heraut, before entering the plain of Tatary, a position established at Bactra (Bulkh), and an Alexandria ad calcem Caucasi south of this range of mountains, near Cabul, which served for military bases in Alexander's demonstrations in Central Asia. The cities built or founded by the conqueror were originally nothing more than fortified camps; and the subsequent wealth and magnificence of these celebrated places, testify the judicious selection of their sites for commercial and military purposes.

probably far beyond the extent *originally* contemplated. The period occupied in the subjugation of the then known world was comprised between the time of his crossing the Hellespont and his return and death at Babylon, viz., from 330 to 323 B. C., in all about seven years. Vast designs for the benefit of mankind were conceived and executed within this brief space in the age of nations. So permanent were these projects in their results, that kingdoms and dynasties started into existence from well-planned schemes, which subsequently endured with the Seleucidæ and the Ptolemies through centuries of time, handing down to posterity the refinements and literature of Greece and Egypt; perpetuating the purposes of benevolence which originated in the divine mind of their immortal founder,—the universal philanthropist no less than universal conqueror.

The remnants of Grecian antiquities still to be found in Central Asia bear witness to the extent of civilization which existed in countries subdued by the remote operations of Alexander's expedition, after the lapse of twenty-two centuries. I have now before me an engraved gem, in the form of a signet, found at Beygram, (site of Alexandria ad calcem Caucasi,) near Cabul, representing the tutelar deity of Athens, in a threefold character, viz.: the patroness of navigation, of war, and of letters. The whole is comprised upon a table no larger than a central section of a split pea: the material a ruby, about the thickness of a playing card, highly polished. The engraving has been done by a few bold strokes of the practised hand of an expert artist: the finest delicacy of tact was necessary to manipulate the mere scale of a substance so extremely fragile. The figure represents Minerva standing on the prow of a boat, armed with helmet, shield, and spear, and bearing the germ of letters near the back of the shoulder, the Greek alpha, which also implies the name of the goddess, Athenæ. The bold and scientific address skilfully exhibited in the execution of the engraving, the polish of the gem, the voluminous design of the representation, indicate the arts, the sciences, the commerce, war, and letters predominant twenty-two centuries ago in the heart of Asia, implanted there by a European philanthropist, in a country now no longer acquainted with the expired empires which numbered its population and ancestry amongst the noblest of the human race, the accomplished progenitors of ancient days. In seven years Alexander performed feats that have consecrated his memory amongst the benefactors of mankind, and impressed the stamp of civilization on the face of the known world, which have commemorated his labours amongst the blessings of a Deity with a deserved though flattering attribution of worshipping votaries.

Turn now to England, and see what she has done for Asia after the military and unmolested possession of the country, the absolute and undisputed administration of the government, legislative and executive, for a period of *eighty* years! England, the zealous friend of the purity of government throughout the universe, the country which arrogates to itself a paramount position amongst the monarchs of this palmy world, the paragon of nations! At this moment, if the Indo-British government was dissolved, and the English were withdrawn from India, there would be left no other memorial of their previous existence than the monuments of their inhumanity,—the barracks, the hospitals, and the jails; the cantonments of their soldiers, the instruments of their tyranny; the hospitals and jails for the victims of their revenue system, their crushing political economy, their irresponsible and despotic sway. No city marks the site of British philanthropy in fated India, but the ruins of villages and depopulated districts show where the griping hand of an English collector has blasted the hopes of a generation. Do we seek for commercial immunities, facilities, or institutions bestowed upon the Indian people, and which may have been rationally anticipated as an expedient measure in a community whose rulers have been called a nation of " shopkeepers ?"—The certainty of temporary possession has cut short prospective legislation, and the destitute apathy of oppressed and plundered millions stand before you in nakedness, hunger, and utter mendicity. Have the arts and civilization of Europe munificently blessed the communities of Asia—the sciences and the *beaux arts* diffused among them? behold a laconic demonstration of the abuses attending on British policy in India.

Slavery, " where the peasant is sold and none to buy," slavery in its cruellest form—forced labour without a patron. Famines, discontent, disaffection, and rebellion, financial distress, fall of prices, reduced revenues, crime abounding, low wages and high interest of money, monopolies of salt, opium, and tobacco. Empire of opinion, might against right, cultivation declining, total absence of internal improvement, no public works, no roads, no canals,*

* The reconstruction of the old canal of Ali Murdaun near Delhi does not impugn the assertion. The solitary and partial exception

no dissemination of knowledge or improvements in education. We see here the consequences of a military despotism; a government imposed upon millions, and sustained by the sword, without a philanthropic motive; originating in cupidity, nourished and developed by tyrannous force, sealed in blood. The tenure of the British rule is a phenomenon unprecedented in the history of mankind, and of wonderful and unexampled interest.

In the beginning, those who now govern India were an association of traders, a band of commercial adventurers, a body of hucksters, natives of a small, contemptible island in the Western Ocean. Having tasted the luxuries of Asia, enjoyed the profits of a voyage to India, and beheld the munificent rivers of wealth which then flowed from exhaustless and untouched sources, these future conquerors, lowly and submissively, with unpretending humility solicited permission of the Indian princes to traffic in their dominions. A factory, purely for the transactions of their trade, was established and tolerated upon the extremest confines of the Moghul's possessions. The feeble Indians simply cherished with hospitable designs the starving snake which was to bask hereafter in their

---

rather proves the unfinished design of impotent enterprise. The British policy is full of ostentatious feints of systematic deception, amongst which the garb of philanthropy is an antique habit. Witness her long-practised anti-slavery doctrines in the West exploded by her grasping and audacious assumption of maritime supremacy; her infamous invasion of Chinese civilization, with the pretext of dispelling the illusions of barbarism amongst a people where, if stability of government and "the greatest happiness of the greatest number" are criterions of judgment, the palm of refinement is unsuccessfully contested by any European nation.

vitals, to batten upon the blood of their people, and fertilize futurity with the plunder of their treasures.

The Indians say they craved only so much land as might be enclosed by a cow's hide; the favour was conferred, and the claimants shred their hide into strings, artfully enclosing a considerable space, upon which a *factory* or rather a fort—for the edifice served both purposes—was quietly reared, and they became for one hundred and fifty years the unmolested possessors of a malignant spot upon the disk of a threatened empire. Other European nations, the Spaniards, the Portuguese, the French and the Dutch, had attempted the experiment of distant dominion. To these people, who anticipated the English in the assumption of political power, our band of adventurers became the object of jealous hostility. Prompted by the successful issue of speculations planned by their European competitors for the political aggrandizement of their respective establishments, the English were stirred to the execution of ambitious projects which invested them with territorial sovereignty; subsequently, the necessity of defending their position involved them in wars of endless conquests. The Indians too late discovered their fatal error; unavailing efforts to drive out the intruders served to strengthen their enemies; they were diverted from defensive measures by internal commotions, and distracted by the crash of the Moghul Empire, which was then in a state of rapid dissolution. Their struggles were enfeebled by domestic divisions; the English, ever ready to avail themselves of these disasters, stimulated the native chiefs, as the princes of India strove for independence, against each other; and carrying out the maxim of "divide et impera," they became the umpires of conflicting governments. Wielding the power thus attained for the prosecution of their original object, as they gradually assumed the supremacy of dominion, and each successive conquest, like a stone thrown into the sea of nations, has expanded the circles of their power, until every part of the Moghul Empire has become subjugated to their sway.

Sir John Malcolm informs us, " the Company were indebted to a physician for the formation of their establishment in Bengal." This was the commencement of their prosperity, and they owed their fortune to a singular accident. A gentleman named Broughton, went from Surat to Agra, where he chanced to cure the daughter of the Emperor Shah Jehan of a severe malady; among the rewards of this benefit, he received the privilege of carrying on a free trade. His medical skill also ingratiated him with the Nawaub of Bengal, who extended the privilege to his nation; and the Company were enabled in 1636 to build a factory at Hoogly. Their medical officers frequently became diplomatic agents, when despatched on professional visits to the Indian princes. On another occasion one of these practised messengers sent to the Emperor Feroksere in 1715, was instructed to solicit exclusive commercial immunities for his nation; in this petition he was successful.* Thus, the foundations of this vast empire

---

* The superior skill of Europeans in medicine, which had first enabled them to obtain a footing in Bengal, now afforded an opportunity of greatly extending their influence. In 1715, under the reign of the Emperor Feroksere, the Presidency sent two factors, with an Armenian merchant, on a commercial mission to Delhi. "The principal object was defeated, but the Emperor happening to labour under a severe illness, which the ignorance of the native physicians rendered them unable to treat with success, was completely cured by a medical gentleman named Hamilton, who ac-

may be inscribed by the voice of fancy, with the record of gratitude due to the professional abilities of a physician. Eighty years have elapsed since the operations of Lord Clive renewed the English power in India, and within that period has the mighty sway been created, which now embraces a great continent, and 140,000,000 vassals subject to the political influence of England. Their system is chiefly managed by a *native* army of about 160,000 well disciplined troops, while the entire military force, composed of British or Europeans, falls short of 30,000; and the estimated number of all the Europeans in India, not in the civil or military service, scarcely reaches three thousand!

companied the embassy. For this signal service he was desired to name his reward. Animated by a patriotic spirit, he asked only privileges and advantages for the Company, and obtained a grant of three villages in the vicinity of Madras, with liberty to purchase in Bengal thirty seven additional townships; an arrangement which would have secured a territory extending ten miles upwards from Calcutta.

"The Emperor granted also the still more important privilege of introducing and conveying their goods through Bengal, without duty or search. But the acquisition of these districts was frustrated by the artful hostility of the Nawaub, who, by private threats deterred the owners from consenting to the purchase. Still the permission of free trade, though limited to foreign exports and imports, proved of the greatest importance, and soon rendered Calcutta a very flourishing settlement."—*Hist. of India*, vol. i. p. 268.

CHAPTER III.

GEOGRAPHICAL BOUNDARIES OF BRITISH INDIA—MORAL AND PHYSICAL CHARACTER OF THE PEOPLE.

THE British power now embraces the whole of that vast region, which extends from Cape Comorin to the mountains of Thibet and the Indian Caucasus, and from the longitude of Heraut to Arracan inclusive, (between 64° and 94° east of London.) By the military occupation of eastern Khorassaun (Avghanistaun) as an impregnable frontier against foreign *European* aggression, imagining their power sufficiently consolidated in Central Asia, they have despatched an armament of European and native troops to open negotiations with the Emperor of China for the establishment of their *commercial relations* with that empire on a firm basis of lasting *friendship!*

A correct knowledge of the moral and physical character of the people inhabiting the Indo-British empire, will lead us to a proper estimate of their military powers, enable us to ascertain their value amongst the race of man, and the rank of their degree in the range of civilization.

The Hindoo and Mussulman population, which

are the principal divisions of the mass, comprises every variety and description of human beings. Some of them intelligent and active, but for the most part oppressed by poverty, sunk into apathy, and debased by revolting ignorance. The bravest and the boldest men may be found in the midst of the timid and abject. The fierce spirit of their turbulent military tribes is untamed. Partially restrained by their conquerors, the unbounded genius of revenge, the self-consuming and the self-existing principle of ambition stimulate their hatred of a foreign race. Impatient and incorrigible, they cherish a profound malignity of aversion to the British yoke. But their efforts to throw off the power that trammels the expansion of dark designs, displays the futility of military enterprise unsustained by social faith. Reciprocal fidelity is the bond of union which confirms the social condition of man, and unity is the key that opens before us the portal to successful results. National mistrust of their native princes, arising from their unstable principles, their infirmity of purpose, their cupidity, and the imbecility of mere physical force opposed to scientific system, generate treason in place of confidence, and to realize their hopes of future independence, a point of concentration is ardently sought after, which shall be antagonist in every attribute to their *European military* oppressors. By the aid of such a power they may achieve the ascendant, and recover the inheritance of their ancestorial rights.

"The native soldier—who are for the most part Hindoos—is shrewd, quick and tractable; facile in his conception, and fond of pre-eminence and military glory; irascible and readily excited, capable when skilfully managed of courageous efforts and enduring patience;" but his physical powers are feeble and unsuited to the moral aptitude of perseverance. Quickly exhausted, he falls an early victim to continued fatigue, and the inclemencies of a cold and novel climate, which would scarcely be regarded by the robust capabilities of an European. The granivorous Indian falling into hopeless, listless insignificance in comparison with the massive-limbed carnivorous consumer of the western hemisphere. The physical temperament of the Hindoos has strongly affected their character, and exhibits prominently their incapability to oppose the robust strength and personal prowess of European troops. "Their make is slender and delicate; their shapes are in general fine; the muscular strength is small, even less than the appearance of their bodies, though expressive of weakness, would lead the spectator to infer. Their stature in general is considerably lower than the European standard, though such inferiority is more remarkable in the south, and diminishes as you advance towards the north. The extreme simplicity and lightness of the aliments used by the Hindoo, and the smallness of his consumption, owing to his sedentary life and the sumptuary laws of his religious system, must undoubtedly have been amongst the causes of the lightness and feebleness of his frame: his food consists almost solely of rice, and his drink is nothing but water. Abstinence and temperance, whilst they generate mutually sustaining each other. His demands are satisfied with a pittance which appears extreme to the people of almost every other part of the world. The prohibition by the Hindoo religion of the flesh of animals for food is not such as to have produced by any means a total abstinence, but the quantity consumed is no doubt small. The luxury of the Hindoo is butter, prepared in a manner peculiar to himself, called by him ghee.

"In Hindostan the people of all sorts are a diminutive race. From the great delicacy of his texture the Hindoo's imagination and passions are easily inflamed, and he has a sharpness and quickness of intellect which seems strongly connected with the sensibility of his outward frame. But though the body of the Hindoo is feeble it is agile in an extraordinary degree. In running and marching they equal, if not surpass, people of the most robust constitutions. Their messengers will go fifty miles a day for twenty or thirty days without intermission. Their infantry, if *totally unincumbered with burthens*, which they could by no means support, will march faster and with less weariness than Europeans. Another remarkable circumstance in the character of the Hindoos, in part too no doubt the effect of corporeal weakness, though in some sort opposite to that excitability which has been remarked, is the inertness of disposition so remarkable to all observers of this peculiar race. The love of repose reigns in India with more powerful sway than in any other region probably of the globe. Listlessness and phlegmatic indolence pervade the inhabitants, who follow the precepts of Brahma. Few pains, to the mind of a Hindoo, are equal to that of bodily exertion; the pleasure must be intense which he prefers to that of its total cessation." This listlessness and apathy is partly the effect of climate and partly the consequence of their political system, the first deteriorating the body, and the latter subduing the intellectual energies. Inanition and oppression bring mendicity and misery in their train. From this condition of life they are relieved by death, and the belief in the transmigration of souls presents the finale of nature in the light of a coveted maturity.

The tyrannical and ruinous system of fiscal policy and bad revenue institutions deprive the peasant of all extraneous wealth accruing from the utmost stretch of labour and leaves merely the miserable portion of *necessary* rations for animal subsistence. —The plan of farming great estates to the Zemindars, who adopt the principle of subletting to the highest bidder to minor labourers, produces precisely the same distressing effects in India as follow the same project of agriculturists in Ireland. Mendicity and the spirit of turbulence, held down by the bayonet, give rise to apathy and listlessness. Thus a government, evil in effect and absolute in form,—a British executive government, without British law, an Oriental despotism,—has riveted the shackles of slavery upon the whole agricultural population of British India.

The working classes,—and here every man is a productive labourer except the usurer (money-lender,)—provide for the luxury of others, and in most instances barely participating in the fruits thereof. And it is a fact, that the inhabitants of extensive districts have been known to subsist on the spontaneous produce of the soil, as grass seeds, potherbs and ground thorns, during several months in the year. The price of one-sixth of a penny sterling (about half a pice) in the quantity of flour necessary for daily subsistence, is a sufficient cause to command and induce the temporary migration of the poor members of a community, from a village whose produce may have suffered from drought, to another more fortunate, though at the distance of several days' journey. Immense crowds of persons who depend upon day-work for their subsistence, are sometimes seen moving through a country in rags or nakedness, flying before the pestilence of threatened famine, whilst pampered luxury prevails in the palaces of their chiefs. The natives of India, subjected to a wretched government, under which the fruits of labour are not secure, are without a motive to work, no less so than the enslaved African for whom the English affect the warmest sympathy.

Interesting impartialness
of the native Indian
although laden with
familiar Oriental
notions of their "Oriental
the govt. Despot". Equally
scathing of the Brit govt.
~~social~~
as the social
inadequacies
seen in India

- Useful bits

- Treatise at beginning
on how a sustainable
colonial govt. must
work to be successful

CHAPTER IV.

FOREIGN RELATIONS OF BRITISH INDIA.

By referring to the foreign relations of the Indo-British empire, we shall instantly see the fragile tenure by which England preserves possession of her Oriental dominions. According to the highest authority it is alone by the bravery and fidelity of the sepoys that India can be preserved to Great Britain. Sir John Malcolm deprecates any accession to the European force, on the ground that it might, from particular causes, weaken the attachment and lessen the efficiency of the native troops; at the same time this very competent judge acknowledges that his countrymen can never succeed in establishing any cordial or social union with their Indian subjects, so widely do they differ in manners, language, religion, and feelings. Other material circumstances contribute to render the British dominion precarious and unique, and to exact the utmost care in the selection of the depositary of that arbitrary power, without which it cannot be prolonged, or even beneficially administered for the rulers or the people.*

* " British government without British law !"

Sir John Malcolm observes: "The only safe view that Great Britain can take of her empire in India, is to consider it, as it really is, always in a state of danger, and to think it quite impossible to render her possessions in that country secure, except under the management of able and firm rulers. If a succession of men of great talents and virtues cannot be found, or if the operation of any influence on party feelings and principles prevents their being chosen, we must reconcile ourselves to the serious hazard of the early decline, if not the loss of the great dominion we have founded in the East."

This was the condition of the British power in India at a time when there was no European rival, or the prospect of an antagonist, on the immense arena of conflicting nations. How has the precarious position of the government been aggravated by the approximation of a hostile power in the Russian military demonstrations and prevalence of her diplomatic influence in Persia, in Central Asia, and the contiguous provinces of India! Considerations of this nature induced the governor-general of India to attempt and effect the military occupation of Avghanistaun. This measure of the Indo-British government is a profound error of policy. Diplomacy and economy condemn the movement, no less than the national safety and defensive plan of operations which the position of India suggests.

It was remarked by a son of Jelall ul Deen, Akber, the greatest of his race who dignified the throne of the Great Moghul, that the fortress of Akberabad was without a ditch. The Emperor replied, "My son, the river Indus is the ditch of Agra." The Indus has always been alleged as the frontier of India, and the laws of Menu prohibit the followers of Bramah from crossing that stream. But the institutes of the reverend Menu are not without the pale of reformation; the god of Menu has been partially displaced from his temples in these degenerate days, and gold is worshipped as the spirit of the age. The conservative and unchanging Brahmin, at the bidding of his golden deity, threw dust in the eyes of Menu, and irreverently disobeyed the laws of his forefathers. The geographical boundary on the west has been crossed; a barrier to the self-protection of India overthrown; new kingdoms have been subdued at an enormous and incredible expense. Extended foreign relations, and the acquisition of strange dominions unconnected with India, require separate establishments, military and civil, for their maintenance; and we have now a portion of the empire of Central Asia to engage our consideration, which is another and an independent Tatar dominion, in no way a part of the Indo-British government, having relations with the surrounding states involving a web of policy that brings back again to Europe the universal sway of England.

A line now drawn from Constantinople to Pekin, (exclusive of Persia,) will divide the East between England and Russia; all to the south falling to the former, whilst the latter emphatically claims and holds the north. By advancing their frontier into Central Asia, the British re-established what has some time been the *political* boundary of India, viz.: the Indian Caucasus; though if this consideration influenced their measures, they should have gone to the river Oxus, which still more frequently has been the political boundary of the Persian or the Indian empire, dividing the Maver ul Neher and Khwarizm of Arabian geographers from the latter.

Unconnected and distant from India, the partially subdued and struggling Avghans still oblige their infidel masters to depend upon their southeastern dominion as a base of action; thus they aggravate the hazard of compromising the safety of their Indian empire, for without elaborating the means of sustaining a large military force in Central Asia, they have incurred the responsibility of defending, from a distant base, liable to interruption from political, and they may be permanent causes, a position, the evacuation of which cannot be proposed without displaying an inferiority to their competitors. The elucidation of this truth would draw upon them the quiescent but not subdued energies of a turbulent and oppressed population. The approach of Russian influence, and the extension of her frontier, places the British government in the dangerous position of being obliged to defend her Indian empire against internal commotion, at the same moment she is necessitated to repel the agression of a foreign power, with whom the means of her defence are physically inadequate to contend! But I am of opinion that the *moral influence* of Russia could extinguish by diplomacy alone the British power in India. Sustained by a military force at Bulkh, the intelligent and astute corps diplomatique of Russia " would excite those causes of fermentation existing there," which would produce " a convulsion within the bosom of the empire," revolutions of opinion, rebellions, insurrections *en masse* of the whole population, war, violence, and devastation, desolating and exterminating the English, and ending in the disintegration of the British empire.

CHAPTER V.

ROUTES INTO INDIA.

By my late expedition into Tatary from Cabul to Bulkh in 1838-39, an enterprise of great magnitude was accomplished. Commanding a division of the Cabul army, and accompanied by a train of artillery, that stupendous range of mountains the Indian Caucasus was crossed through the Paropamisus. The military topography and resources of the country were practically tested. Impediments which were supposed to present insurmountable obstacles to the passage of an army, proved to be difficulties readily vanquished by labour and perseverance, and the practicability of invading India from the north, no longer doubtful, has become a feasible and demonstrable operation.

To follow the system of Alexander, Bulkh, the ancient Bactra, should be made the base of action of every military movement against India. Bulkh is the capital of Central Asia, morally and politically; and the power holding possession of this far-famed city,—which is supposed by the Orientals to have been the first built, thence called Mader i Bulad, or the Mother of Cities,—would be enabled to exercise over the superstitious natives a supremacy

AVGHANISTAUN. 81

which it is an article of their faith to number amongst the fated incidents of their race, viz., the predominance of Christian policy over the kingdoms of all the earth;—and one of the signs which mark the approach of this period, is indicated by the re-edification of Bulkh, which is again to flourish, according to their traditions, as the capital of Central Asia.

The resources of the Uzbeck States have sustained the armies of a conqueror, who we are told by history plundered both Delhi and Moscow (whose descendant still occupies the throne of Pekin), and whose dynasty has, within the last eighty years, been removed from the throne of Delhi! The greatest military empires that ever existed, not inferior even to the Russian of this age, or rather *day*, strove for predominance on the Uzbeck plains, and ruled alternately at Bulkh, at Samerkand, or Ghiznee; respectively, the empire of Darius Hystaspes, the empire of Timour, and of Abastagi, or Mahmoud. These expired empires, no longer claiming military distinction in the grade of nations, have become purely agricultural and pastoral, and adequate to the maintenance of military array now as when under the sway of Darius Hystaspes,* of Chagati, of Timour, and Mahmoud. Numberless hosts have contested for mastery upon

* In the reign of Darius Hystaspes the celebrated Zoroaster promulgated at Bulkh or Bactra the religious system of the Fire-Worshippers, and in this place a great temple was founded and dedicated to the Sun. At present every remnant of antiquity has disappeared from superficial inspection, and no vestiges of the former existence of a Grecian or Persian city are now visible, although the uneven surface of the ground in the vicinity of the modern town, would probably disclose beneath its mounds indications of former days.

6

these plains, and nation following nation from the far and mysterious East, have poured forth their migratory hordes over this great thoroughfare of the world to conquer and to colonize the wastes of Europe with Tatar blood,* and prove the fruitfulness of Central Asia.†

Those golden-sanded rivers, the Oxus and Jaxartes, penetrate far into the interior of the Uzbeck States, and connect their remotest provinces with the great commercial depot of Astrakhan in southern Russia, and ultimately with Moscow: they ensure the necessary capabilities for strategical demonstrations. Whilst the political divisions and internal dissensions of the country invite the regard of Russia, the geography multiplies the facilities of accomplishing all that an invading power could aspire to hope. To ascertain the probabilities of success in any enterprise, we should examine the facts and attend to the results attained under corresponding circumstances. Reviewing the causes and consequences connected with the adventures of antecedent conquerors of India, we may observe, that this country, though it has frequently been subjugated, has always been subdued, until the advent of British ascendancy, by an invasion from the north; and it is an undoubted fact, that each individual who signalized his name by an inroad into, or aggrandized his empire by annexing India to his dominions, consummated his views through similar if not precisely the same plan of operations. Abstracting from the account of available references the antiquated and problematic intimations of India derived from scriptural allusions

---

* The Huns, the Alemanni, the Turks and Moghuls, &c. &c.
† The Uzbeck States.

in the days of Ezekiel (xxvii. 23), the fabulous mythology of Bacchus, and the no less doubtful traditions of Sesostris and Semiramis, we assume with Herodotus the authenticated records of history, which point to Darius Hystaspes as the first successful invader of India, whose inroads were attended by permanent results. When India formed one of the twenty satrapies of Persia, Bactra was the capital of Darius, a city upon the site of which we have now the modern town of Bulkh; and it was from this position of the central province of the Sun, that Darius, having previously ascertained by the expedition of Scylax the feasibility of his own ambitious designs, attempted and effected the conquest of India. Subsequently, Alexander claimed India as a province of Persia, as partially appears from Quintus Curtius. Having overrun the whole of the Persian empire as far as the river Jaxartes, he established a government and cantoned his army for awhile at Bulkh, and finding Persia every where subdued and submissive, he crossed the Paropamisus and completed the subjugation of the known world by the conquest of India. Bulkh was his base of action on the north of the Paropamisian range. There is a gorge opening into the valley of Cabul near Seri Chushma, at the debouche of the pass of Onai, descending from the north, which is called at this day "Dahun i Secundereah," or debouche of Alexandria. From this incident it may be inferred the valley of Cabul was probably known to the Greeks as the province of Alexandria, and that Beygram was the site of the city of Alexandria ad calcem Caucasi. This position was one of the intermediate points of communication between Bactra and Attock, the chain being completed by

Nysia—supposed to have been founded by Bacchus, now called Ningrahar or Djilallabad—and Peshour, the Peucalaotes* of the Greeks. Alexandria ad calcem Caucasi, as may be seen by inspection of the map, commands the debouche of the route over the Hindoo Kush, via Ghorebund, and also that by Panjshare. The western extremity of the plain, called Koh damum, in which the ancient city stood, commands the Bameean route at the gorge of Secundereah. The city being placed on the eastern side of the plain, in the vicinity of the difficult moun-

* Peucalaotes—This term evidently means Peshour; for if we cut off the Greek termination, which their writers were accustomed to add to the names of localities, we have Peucola. Now in the Avghan pronunciation the s in Peshour is pronounced k, and we have Peukola. The l is represented by r in languages which are deficient in the liquid, as the Chinese: where the l does not exist, The r is always substituted; and you are sometimes offered a very unsaleable commodity by a Chinaman who proposes to dispose of a bag of rice. The sound of l and r when occurring in the middle division of a word is scarcely distinguishable, and those who lisp or have otherwise an impediment in their speech, invariably say one for the other, so that by this process of derivation, without violating orthography, we have the modern Peshour distinctly representing the Greek Peucalaotes. By a similar mode of derivation we have the modern Ab-i-Cheen, Ab-i-Sinai, or Ascessines; and Ravee from Hydraotes or Hydravotes, the first syllable signifying river or water, the third place or locality, the second the native Indian name. The Byas, Bias, Beeas or Veas, is the Hyphasis. The Sutledge, Sudless, Sudruss, Sudledge, is the *Hysudrus*, making Sudless without the Greek prefix. The name of *Hydaspes* comes from the compound of river and horse in the Greek and Persian languages. The appellation was probably conferred in consequence of the death of Bucephalus, who was killed in the battle with Porus or Poorun, as he is called in Indian annals, which was fought upon the plain bordered on its west by the *Hydaspes*, in the modern jurisdiction of Guzerath, of which I was both civil and military governor for several years when in the service of his highness Maha Rajah Runjeet'h Singh, Prince of the Panjab.

tain passes towards Ghorebund, or Gholebund,* as it is colloquially pronounced, Panjshare, Tugao Saffi, and Tazeen, to restrain the wild hordes of those alpine districts, whilst it also overruled and garrisoned the plain.

After the death of Alexander, Bactria, which included Avghanistaun, fell to Seleucus, and shortly after the decline of the Syrian kingdom, became an independent state, governed by Grecian rulers, and continued several ages a powerful and enlightened dominion.

The history of this period is involved in darkness, and the only elucidation which can now be ascertained has lately been laid open by interesting and important discoveries in numismatology. Coins, which are the representatives of expired nations, now illuminate the mysterious history of the Bactrian empire, denoting to modern investigation its extent and power. Under Menander, some of whose coins are now in my possession, Bactria was bounded on the north by the river Jaxartes, on the south by the Indian ocean; and the conquests of this prince passed the Hyphasis on the east. The western boundary was probably the Caspian Sea. It was after the duration of nearly two hundred years that the irruption of barbarous conquerors from the North, the Chagatæ or Getæ, and the rise of the Parthian empire, put an end to the kingdom of Bactria (page 49–50, Hist. of India.)

India was invaded by the Parthian prince, Mithri-

* Gholebund signifies *spirit's prison*, and it is a singular coincidence that the immense and undefined cave at Finjan is known in Sancrit lore as the cave of Promet'h, and is doubtless the locality called by the Greeks the cave of Prometheus, near which, we are told, was situated the city of Alexandria ad calcem Caucasi.

dates, but his expedition was probably a temporary inroad, as we are not aware of any permanent Parthian domination in India. Coins of the Sassanadian dynasty are numerous and frequently found in extensive deposits, adventitiously disclosed by the agricultural labours of individuals. They have been brought to view by the plough or the spade in considerable deposits, contained in earthen pots. A treasure of this kind was brought to Dost Mahomed, who despatched the coins to the mint, where the *melting pot* shortly renewed their currency. The Persians of Artaxerxes also penetrated far beyond the Indus. The coins of Julius Cæsar and Mark Antony, with other rare antiquities of the Romans, have been found at Mankyallah in the Panjab.

In the year 873 Ismael Samani of Bocharah assumed the title of king, and after nearly one hundred years the decline of his dynasty and a disputed succession enabled Abastagi, governor of the province of Khorassaun, Bulkh being his capital, successfully to raise the standard of insurrection. Becoming an independent sovereign, located at Bulkh, *he added to his domain* the high mountain territory of Cabul and Kandhar. The Avghans were a nation of hardy shepherds, husbandmen, and warriors, who have often extended the authority of their princes over the surrounding countries. Here Abastagi selected Ghiznee as the capital of an empire which long ruled over Asia. From this period—977, A. D.—we have authentic Mahomedan records of Indian history, by which we are made acquainted with the revolutions of dominion endured by the natives of that country. The successors of Abastagi, in 997, A. D., subdued the representative of the Samanian dynasty, who ruled in

Bocharah. Mahmoud,* the son of Sebuctagi,† joined with the King of the Uzbecks in extinguishing the empire of Bocharah, and the fine territory of Maver ul Neher (Transoxiana) was added to his dominion, which then comprehended all Asia, from the Caspian Sea to the Indus. In the reign of Masaood, who succeeded Mahmoud, the migratory conquests of the Turks under the Seljukian dynasty overran Khorassaun, and the successors of the Ghuznevide contended in vain with Toghrul, who subverted the throne of Bagdad, and was installed by Ul Keim, the last of the Khuleefas (caliphs), vicegerent of the Prophet. He was followed by Alp Arslan, that just and gallant warrior, who wrote upon his tomb at Mer'w, "Ye who have seen the glory of Alp Arslan exalted to the heavens, come and see it buried under the dust." The monarchs of Ghiznee saw wrested from them the fine plains of Khorassaun and Iraun—even that of Bulkh —and their dominion confined within the mountain barrier of the Caucasus. To the Toorks, whose inroads into India were commemorated by the nuptial bonds of Alp Arslan's heir with the house of Ghiznee, the Ghorian monarchs succeeded.

This dynasty was also derived from the North. The Ghorian princes sprang from a race of hardy mountaineers who inhabited the highest arable altitudes of the Paropamisus, now called Yenghore, near Bameean. Mahmoud of Ghoree obtained the government of Ghiznee in 1174. He invaded India through Mooltaun and Ajmeer, consequently, to reach the last named place, he passed through *the*

* In 997.
† Called by Mahomedan historians Sebuktageen. He was the General of Abastagi. He ascended the throne of Ghiznee in 977.

Great Western Desert, which separates Rajpootana from Scind and Bhawulpore.

Two campaigns were fought with Scythian valour; the victories of the last repairing the disasters of the first, ended in the tumultuary flight and irredeemable discomfiture of the Indian army. The King of Delhi fell, and his empire became the prey of the Moslems, whose dominion was for the first time established in the heart of India. Mahomed returned to Ghuznee by the way of Lahore, leaving his lieutenant, Kuttub, to maintain his authority in that quarter. He was murdered on the banks of the Indus, near Attock, by the Guickwars, and the dynasty of Ghoree fell with him. His lieutenants, Ildecuz in Ghuznee, and Kuttub in Delhi, soon erected for themselves independent sovereignties. Kuttub ul Deen was the founder of the Avghan or Patan dynasty, which continued from 1210 to the invasion and conquest of Baber the Moghul in 1525. The rule of the Patan dynasty was disturbed by the invasion of Timour the Tatar, known in oriental history by the cognomen of Timourleng; he claimed descent from Chungez. Timour conquered Delhi, but retained no acquisitions in India. His attention was drawn off by distant operations in Persia, and the west, Constantinople then being besieged by Byazeed (Bajazet). He was a native of Kokand or Ferghana, and after his death his immense dominions falling to pieces, this province of Kokand was all that remained to his descendant Baber. Those conquerors also penetrated into India, via Cabul, crossing the Paropamisus from Bulkh. Of Timour it is said, " he set out from Samarkand (the Marakanda of Q. Curtius) in 1397, and advanced without difficulty along the immense plains of Bactria. Then he had to scale the tremendous barrier of the Indian Caucasus," &c. Subsequent to Baber, India was invaded by his son Humaioon, who had been dethroned and exiled. After residing several years at the Court of Persia, he regained his crown through the countenance of Shah Tamasp, who had maintained him with regal munificence. The King of Persia provided him with ten thousand men, and presented him with Cabul in Jaghire, on condition of his embracing the sectarian faith of Persia—that sect, called Sheah, viewed as schismatics by the orthodox Mahomedans. This stipulation, which the Indian prince seems never to have violated, accounts for the prevalence of the Sheah sect in India, all the Mahomedan rulers of which empire were of the Suni or orthodox persuasion, until the reign of Humaioon. Receiving Cabul as a free gift from the King of Persia, he immediately added Kandhar to his possessions by treachery: thus returning the munificence of Shah Tamasp by an act of ingratitude und unthankful depravity. Internal rebellions frequently disturbed the peace of India, and the monarch, when obliged to yield to the adverse fortune of war, usually retreated to Cabul as a place of temporary refuge, where, gathering strength from the military population, they again subjected India to their sway.

Nadir Shah, the Persian invader of India, in 1736 conquered Avghanistaun. It is said he *first* subdued Cabul and then reduced Kandhar. It is certain a division passed from Bulkh to Cabul, as I have been informed by the Uzbeck Prince of Khoolum, Mahomed Amir Beg Meer i Wallee, from whom I received the traditional lore of Nadir's inroad. Nadir saw what the sagacity of Lord Auckland could not penetrate, that India and Persia could not be united in one kingdom; and contenting himself with exacting from the King of Delhi, when the Indian empire lay prostrate at his feet, as he stood upon the ruins of its plundered capital, the cession of Cabul, Kandhar, and all the provinces, as a part of Persia, west of the Indus,—which river is known to be the geographical though not always the political boundary of India,—he reseated the King of Delhi anew upon his throne, giving him much salutary advice, and retreated across the Indus, never leaving a soldier or retaining a fortified post in Hindoostan. Eight years after this event Nadir was assassinated at Meshud in Khorassaun, and an Avghan, named Ahmed Abdalhee, being joined by the Avghan troops in Nadir's service, hastily returned to Kandhar, where he seized a great treasure on the way from India to Persia, and was proclaimed King of Avghanistaun by the coalition of a few principal chiefs of his native country. Ahmed Shah was the first of the Dooraunee monarchs. In 1747 he invaded India, defeated the Mahrattas, who then overran the Moghul empire, and entered Delhi as a conqueror.

"It was easy for the victorious Avghan to seat himself on the *vacant* throne of the Moghul, but he seems not to have felt any ambition for this high dignity. Perhaps he was sensible that amidst such a general agitation throughout Hindoostan as then prevailed, and with so many *nations* in arms, such an acquisition *was too distant from Cabul*, the centre of his dominions, to be retained with advantage. Contenting himself with the provinces *west of the Indus*, he quitted in a few months the seat of government, leaving there Alligohur, eldest son of

Allumgeer the II., in possession of the empty, but still venerated title of Great Moghul, to be the tool or become the captive of the first daring chief who should seize the capital."

After this period Hindoostan was relieved from foreign invasion. The preparations of Shah Zemaun, the grandson of Ahmed, in conjunction with Tippoo Sooltaun, for a simultaneous attack upon the English, the Avghans pouring down 100,000 cavalry from the north, whilst Tippoo, under the patronage of Napoleon's policy, advanced from the south, terminated prematurely. The King of Cabul was distracted by rebellions at home, and the invasion of the province of Bulkh, which formed a part of his dominion, by the King of Bocharah, drew off his attention from India, and released the English from the dread of this threatened formidable invasion, instigated by the intrigues of France and Tippoo. Shah Zemaun penetrated into Lahore on several expeditions to levy tribute upon that province, which was a reluctant dependency of his empire. Runjeet'h[*] Singh was then a young adventurer, just commencing life, with a thousand mounted retainers at his heels. For services rendered on one of these expeditions, probably the last, Shah Zemaun conferred upon Runjeet'h the gift of Lahore in feudal tenure. Lahore was then in the possession of Runjeet'h's enemies, who were too powerful to be immediately dislodged, and he was unable to enter into possession, but the document gave a claim which circumstances subsequently enabled him to enforce, and his conquest of the city of Lahore laid the foundations of his

---

[*] Rannajeet'h, or King of Lions.

future fortunes. When Runjeet'h had partially consolidated the Panjab government by the union of many petty tribes, states, and principalities, he frequently made annual predatory demonstrations across the Sutledge as far as Sirhind, plundering the territories between the river and that frontier of the English. In 1809 Sir Charles Metcalfe, by order of the British government, made a treaty with Runjeet'h, which confined his military operations to the right bank of the river Sutledge, but left him at liberty to extend his ambitious projects towards the territories beyond the Sutledge.

The late expedition of the English into Avghanistaun has again placed the Moghul empire under the dominion of one paramount power. These historical references indicate the accessible points of India, and they prove that every conqueror who directed the march of enterprise against India came from the north, established a military base at Bulkh, and advanced by Cabul.

It is upon Bulkh that all the roads debouch, advancing from the south; and it is upon Cabul all the passes into India concentrate, advancing from the north. Heraut and Kandhar are upon the great caravan route from Central Asia to the Deccan or *South* of India. That route, though annually travelled by *commercial* adventurers, has less frequently been the channel of *military* operations. A part of this route is in the line of *indirect* communication between Persia and Cabul, the division of it from Heraut to Kandhar: from that city it branches off northeast towards Cabul. There is a great commercial highway of nations from Constantinople to Pekin, and from Moscow to Delhi.

AVGHANISTAUN. 93

Bulkh is the central or intersecting point upon these routes, and has always been the military and political *capital of Asia*, whether swayed by Persian or Greek, by Parthian, Toork, or Moghul. Upon this position every strategical operation against India must be based to command a fair prospect of success and permanent results.

Here, Harlan uses a number of Northern invaders, amongst them Darius Hystaspes, Alexander, Mithridates, Mahmoud of Ghazni, Timour, Humayun, Nadir Shah, and Shah Zeman would have made an attempt had unity in the North not begun to disintegrate.

— Ultimately, he insists Balkh is the ideal point from which to threaten India.

CHAPTER VI.

REFERENCES FROM ENGLISH AUTHORITIES ON THE FOREIGN RELATIONS OF BRITISH INDIA.

The present political condition of the neighbouring countries surrounding British India, viz.: Beloochistaun, Avghanistaun, Bulkh, Panjab, Nepaul, Birmah, and China, and also the foreign relations of the Indo-British government, may be readily gathered from the annexed copious extracts, the issue of the Indian press. The information thus elicited will, it is supposed, place in a strong light the dubious position of the English in India, and their uneasy tenure of the country.

The anxious fears of the Indian government before the result of the expedition to Cabul transpired; the frantic exultation succeeding a state of despondency when the achievement of an *uncontested* victory gave a transient truce to those well-founded terrors; the thanks of Parliament after the campaign, strongly indicate the danger which threatened the empire, even from the far distant reverberations of the rumours of a Russian war. But the retreat of the Shah of Persia from Heraut reanimated the quailing English, and respited them from those ominous anticipations, which proved the indefensible state of *British* India, and demonstrated the easy conquest awaiting a bold and fearless enemy, characterized by dexterous policy and diplomatic skill.

Extracts from the Indian press, and other authentic English sources, illustrating the foreign relations of the British power in India.

March 29th, 1838.—" The relations between Calcutta and Ava cannot continue on their present unsatisfactory footing. Our attention is so exclusively required for the northwest, (that is, Cabul,) where the web of political combinations, extending from the Panjab to Circassia, appears to grow more complicated, that we cannot afford to allow any insecurity on our eastern boundary. All idea of a war, however, for the next six months, is out of the question. We shall not a second time, commit the incomparable folly of landing an army at Rangoon at the commencement of the rains, but the next cold season should not be allowed to pass over, without a decisive effort to place our intercourse with Ava upon so satisfactory a basis, as to enable us to leave our eastern frontier with confidence under the safeguard of our ordinary troops."

April 13th.—" It is proposed, by taking up an imposing attitude on our frontiers, to inspire the Birmese court with a wholesome awe, which may repress their hostile intentions. We shall be happy to find that these precautionary measures are efficacious in preventing the horrors of war. No man of common humanity would for a moment dream of advocating a war, except as it appeared to be the shortest path to a solid and lasting peace. It is said that the new king will not commence a war with the English, unless some tempting occasion should arise. His object is gained for the present, if we allow him to banish the resident, to trample on the treaty of Yandaboo, and to insult the Governor-General with impunity. [His future efforts will be confined to the disturbance of our frontiers, and to such annoyance of our subjects as may weaken their confidence in us.] He is not perhaps so much inclined for war as his court and the Birmese nobility in general are, but the Birmese, humbled for the first time since the days of Alompra, by the treaty of Yandaboo, thirst to regain their lost honour. We may therefore consider it as not so much probable as certain, that whenever we may be engaged in hostilities in any part of India, we shall inevitably have a Birmese war on our hands also. These transactions cannot fail to affect our position in Asia. For the first time since the battle of Plassey, we have received, instead of dictating the law. [This is the first instance in which a British resident has been expelled from a court, the sanctity of treaties disregarded, and the authority of the Governor-General derided, without being followed by an immediate declaration of war. We must be cautious how we accustom the natives of Asia to the spectacle of our degradation.] We know, that an intercourse has already been opened between Nepaul and Ava; and we should not be surprised to find the example which has now been set, literally followed by the court of Catmandhoo."

June 14th.—"In the year 1815, during the war betwixt the Indo-British government and Nepaul, numerous solicitations had been addressed by the Gorkha Rajah to the Emperor of China. We then find Umer Singh, the Nepaul military chief, strongly recommending to his master to make an urgent appeal to the court of Pekin for assistance, and submitting the proposed draft of an address to that effect. In this he invokes the active co-operation of the high and mighty emperor, on the grounds of the insult that had been offered to his supremacy by the English, in daring to invade a country owing allegiance to, and enjoying the protection of the Chinese government. The attack upon Nepaul is declared to be only a preliminary step to the invasion of Bootan and Thibet, and to securing the passes into the frontiers of China. The wealth and military resources of the British, the fact of their having conquered every prince in the plains, and having afterwards seated themselves on the throne of the Emperor of Delhi, are duly dwelt upon. In conclusion, he points out the readiest means of affording effective aid to their cause, to be the immediate advance of a loan of money for the maintenance of the Gorkha army, and the sending a force of 200,000 or 300,000 Chinese troops through the Dharma territory, that is, Dargeeling, into the lower provinces of Bengal, 'to spread alarm and consternation among the Europeans.' 'Consider,' says he, 'if you abandon your dependants, that the English will soon be masters of Lassa.'

"After the commencement of hostilities, a communication from the Governor-General, cautioning the Chinese, in common with all other neighbouring states, against aiding or abetting the enemies of the British government, reached the Umbas at Shigatze, and awakened considerable apprehensions in their minds.] The original document was immediately forwarded to Pekin, and with it an application from the Rajah of Nepaul for assistance against the invaders. The Emperor is reported to have been highly indignant at the tone and the language assumed by the Marquis of Hastings, and after listening to the memorial of his officers to have exclaimed, 'these English seem to look upon themselves as kings, and upon me as merely one of their neighbouring rajahs.' Orders were forthwith issued for a commission, composed of a Tseankeun and two other Tajin, to proceed under a military escort into the vicinity of the seat of war, to institute inquiries; and an army was ordered to march with all speed after them for the protection of the frontier line. This must have been the force, to whose arrival on the confines of the Chinese territories allusion is made in an official letter from Tytalia, dated June 1816. About this time, three Chinese officers, who styled themselves the Governors of Arzing, addressed a letter to the Governor-General of India, through the medium of the Sikkim Rajah, a prince who was closely connected with the Deb Rajah and the Lama of Lassa, who had shown himself a staunch ally of the British government. In this address, the Chinese officers, after stating the insinuations regarding the ulterior views of the British government, that had been made against them by the Gorkha Rajah, proceeded thus: 'Such absurd measures appear quite inconsistent with the usual wisdom of the British; it is probable they never made the declarations imputed to them: if they did, *it will not be well*. An answer should be sent, as soon as possible, stating whether or not the English ever entertained such absurd propositions; if they did not, let them write a suitable explanation to the Tseankeun, that he may report to the Emperor.' By the same opportunity was received a letter from the Sikkim Rajah, who stated, that the Gorkha Rajah had been trying to impose on the Cheen Rajah, with a story of the Europeans having united with him to attack and conquer Nepaul and China, and this was the sole reason of the Cheen (Chinese) Rajah writing to the Governor-General. In reply, the Governor-General disclaimed any hostile intentions towards China."

In the treaty of peace which soon followed with the Nepaulese, an article was inserted which provided for the residence of a British agent at Catmandhoo, and was with difficulty stomached by the Gorkha cabinet; and it was hoped that the Chinese government might be prevailed on to exert themselves to prevent the establishment of European influence in their neighbourhood. The following narrative of an audience given to the Nepaulese Sirdars, who visited Shigatze for the above purpose, shows clearly enough, that having once got rid of their alarm regarding the advance of the English troops, the Chinese authorities had now become mainly solicitous to uphold the honour and dignity of their country by stopping the mouths of these men, who appealed to them for protection, and pointedly inquired what the world would say if the Emperor of China should abandon his tributaries and dependants to their fate? The narrative proceeds thus:

Scene—Shigatze; a garden-house near the city. "With the Tseankeun (generalissimo) were the two Tajin, seated in chairs, and all the subordinate officers of various ranks stood around them, with their hands joined before them, as if in the act of supplicating. The Nepaulese Sirdars, having previously obtained permission to be attended by their armed escort of 111 men, proceeded to the residence, marching by files in slow order. When they approached the Tseankeun, the whole saluted him after the Chinese manner, by falling on their knees, from which position they arose by an order. During the visit, the Chinese brought out a painting containing likenesses of several of the old officers of the court of Nepaul, and compared them with those present, but only found the likeness of one of the chieftains now before them," &c. The Nepaulese, entering upon the subject of their mission, requested a letter to the English that would induce them to quit Nepaul. The Chinese rejoined, " You have already told us that the English first entered your country for the sole purpose of *establishing a warehouse there*, and upon what plea can we attempt to remove merchants, for such people are not molested in any country whatever?" One of the Sirdars answered, " If they were merely merchants, it would be of no consequence, but they are soldiers and commanders, and what connexion have troops with merchants?" The Tseankeun resumed, " The English have written to inform us that they sent their resident with your own consent; of what then have you to complain? As to what your rajah stated about the English having demanded of him the roads through Bootan, with the intention of penetrating into China, it is false; and if they had any such views, they would find less circuitous routes." The Sirdars remained perfectly silent, and the Tseankeun then addressed himself in a strain of irony to Runbeer. " You Gorkhas think there are no soldiers in the hills but what are in Nepaul. Pray at what do you number your fighting men? and to what amount do you collect revenue? The latter I suppose cannot exceed two lacs!" Runbeer replied, that the number of the soldiers was about that mentioned by the Tseankeun, and that their revenue amounted to about five lacs of rupees per annum. "You are indeed then," said the Tseankeun, "a mighty people," &c. They were dismissed without accomplishing the object of their mission. Unable to ward off the infliction of a British resident, and unwilling to break off their connexion with the Chinese government, the envoys returned to Catmandhoo little satisfied with their reception, and apparently harbouring some vague apprehensions of the design of the "Cheen Maha Rajah." These seem to have been subsequently strengthened, for not long after, we find the Nepaulese minister applying to the British resident for a promise of support in the event of an attack from the Chinese. The establishment of a resident, a British officer, at the court of a prince who owed allegiance and paid homage to the court of China, was a source of considerable vexation to them; the recognition of their supremacy was in a manner compromised, and they were quite prepared to act on the prayer of the Gorkhas, and to use their best endeavours to procure the withdrawal of the newly appointed resident, provided this could be accomplished without their committing themselves with the English, or placing their government in a position which might on a future day lead to collision. Accordingly, in the December following, we hear of a deputation of fifty Sirdars from the Sikkim Rajah, escorting a letter from the Tseankeun and his colleagues, to the Governor-General, together with a box of presents. After stating the high degree of satisfaction they had derived from the frank explanation of the Governor-General, their despatch proceeds as follows:

"His imperial majesty, who, by God's blessing, is well informed of the conduct and proceedings of all mankind, reflecting on the good faith and wisdom of the English Company, and the firm friendship and constant commercial intercourse which has so long subsisted between the two nations, never placed any reliance on the calumnious imputations put forward by the Gorkha rajah." The letter concludes with these words: "You mention that you have stationed a vakeel in Nepaul; this is a matter of no consequence, but as the rajah, from his youth and inexperience, and from the novelty of the circumstance, has imbibed suspicions, if you would, out of kindness towards us, and in consideration of the ties of friendship, withdraw your vakeel, it would be better; and we should feel inexpressibly grateful to you."

The Governor-General replied by pointing out the necessity of stationing an officer at head-quarters, who could always be ready to afford explanations upon matters which might otherwise lead to misunderstanding, and create ill-will. He attributed the late war to the absence of such a person, and then continued: "The habits of the borderers, both of the Nepaulese and the British territory, are rough and violent, hence frequent outrages may occur; but if there were stationed at Catmandhoo any accredited agent of the Emperor of China, to whom this government could with confidence recur upon all matters of dispute arising between it and the

Nepaulese, we should be relieved from the necessity of keeping a resident there at a considerable expense. As the case actually stands, the presence of a British officer is the main security we have for avoiding differences; this officer will be instructed to confine himself to the single care of preserving harmony between the two states, and to abstain from all other interference in the internal or foreign affairs of Nepaul." The last proposition was received with dissatisfaction; in reply, " We advert," say they, " to that part of your letter which desires us to urge our august sovereign, the Emperor of China, to the appointment of a minister at Catmandhoo, to whom your people and those of Nepaul might refer their affairs, and thus prevent disagreements. Be it known to you, that the Gorkha Rajah has long been a faithful tributary of the Chinese government, and refers himself to it whenever occasion requires. There is therefore no need of deputing any one thither from this empire: besides, by the grace and favour of God, his majesty, possessing the sovereignty of the whole kingdom of China, and other parts, does not enter the city of any one without cause. If it so happen that his victorious forces take the field, in such case, after punishing the refractory, he in his royal clemency restores the transgressor to his throne. We have not thought it our duty to represent the point to the court of China, as the matter in question is opposed to the custom of this empire. The frequenters of the port of Canton, which lies within our territory, can inform your lordship that such is not the custom of China; for the future, a proposition of this nature, so contrary to usage, should not be introduced into a friendly despatch."

June 21st. " The contemplation of the anomalous

nature of our government, the entire absence of all community and identity of interests between the government and its subjects, cannot fail to create impressions, calculated to convince the most sceptical mind, that our existence depends exclusively upon the character of our rule, and the energy of our measures. So far as the first is concerned, it is of so mixed a nature, having so much to elicit feelings of unthankfulness and a desire for change in the minds of our subjects generally, that it becomes a perplexing and difficult matter to decide whether the great mass of the people would derive benefit or sustain injury by our removal. The evil that exists under the exclusive nature of our system is prolific in engendering every feeling prompting to desire a change. The consequence is, that restlessness, discontent, and a desire for change may be considered to pervade the whole extent of our dominion, from the Sutledge to the sea, and from the Indus to the Berhampooter, whilst beyond these limits we are looked upon with strong feelings of envy, distrust, and apprehension. Hence we may fairly infer, that the internal and external feeling bear that affinity towards each other which would readily subdue every obstacle tending to prevent the coalescence of our enemies and our subjects for the subversion of our power."

Monday, June 18th.—" An envoy from the Nepaulese court, Runbeer Singh, passed through Lahore on his way to Kandahar."

[August 30th.—" Upon the question of encamping a British army at Cabul—of extending our boundary not to, but beyond the Indus—we have not sufficiently recovered from our surprise at the boldness of the step to be able to look at it with calm consideration.

If we proceed to Cabul, we must maintain ourselves there. We cannot afford a retrograde movement through any emergency of circumstances. If we are forced to recede one step, we must recede two, and so on till the mighty spirit which overspreads India, shrinks back to the narrow dimensions of the barrel, and the empire is reduced to its original element of a factory. At Cabul we must be every thing or nothing. In no transaction in which we mingle in India can we any longer act a secondary part. Are we prepared for that extension of our connections which shall enable us to keep due watch and ward at the gate of India? We have not the Indus for our boundary, and yet we seem about to involve ourselves in a world of new combinations and intrigues beyond that limit, with the Panjab in our rear, more consolidated than any native power since the days of Hyder, and with two unsubdued hollow allies on our northern and eastern frontier to take advantage of the first embarrassment to pour a stream of desolation on our provinces."

October 25th.—"The real object of the present expedition is to establish a lasting barrier against hostile intrigue and aggression by the military occupation of Cabul; that is, to baffle the intrigues and arrest the aggression of Russia, and to anticipate her views by the extension of British influence in Central Asia. The necessity of this movement is indicated by the ill-concealed designs of our real opponent.

"When we look at the strides which our power has taken in India we draw back with astonishment. It is but eighty-two years since our only possession in Bengal consisted of a miserable fortification, garrisoned by seventy European soldiers. Now the army of the Bengal Presidency is about to cross the Indus to establish the just influence of the British government upon a proper footing, amongst the nations of Central Asia. It is only eighty years since Clive, having recovered that fortification, and after having given the English anew a local habitation and a name in Bengal, uttered this memorable sentence: 'We cannot stop here, we must go forward!'—and forward indeed we have gone, year after year, east, west, north, and south, till in the year 1838, the safety of our empire in India demands that an army should march five hundred miles beyond the Indus to raise the siege of Herat'h!"

November 22d.—"We must be in possession of Rangoon and all Pegue before the first of May next."

"There are other considerations besides the defence of the provinces exposed to Birmese invasion, which must go to the formation of a correct judgment on this subject. We know that the publication through the Durpun* (for a copy of which the court of Catmandhoo subscribes,) of the contempt with which the English have been treated from time to time by the Chinese authorities at Canton, has produced a very unfavourable impression on the minds of the Nepaulese, and led them to believe that we are not after all the first power in Asia. In a higher degree must the conduct of the Birmese court towards us, if it be not apologized for or resented, contribute to shake that empire of opinion which we hold in India. The safety of the empire demands that we should vindicate our honour, by pacific means if possible, but still that we should vindicate our honour from those insults, which are offered only under the idea that our

* A native paper.

empire has passed its prime, and that our sun is setting in the East."

November 22d.—" It may be doubted if at any time since we took possession of territory in India, such deep and dangerous disaffection has prevailed as exists at present. Our unsparing taxation, our long continued and augmenting exhaustion of the resources of the country, our resumptions of rent-free lands, our reduction of establishments and of public expenditure, our schemes of conversion under the mask of education and the pretext of non-interference with religious ceremonials, have spread and are spreading throughout India universal alarm and discontent. The political horizon is equally overcast. Both on the west and the east, the faint flashes of an approaching tempest have already been displayed, and if the storm once burst on either quarter, it will immediately fall upon us with fury from the other. Engaged in hostilities with Persia backed by Russia; with Ava, which has already insulted us; and with Nepaul, preparing, if report be true, most vigorously, to recover its lost power and possessions, we shall soon be entangled in a plentiful crop of domestic embarrassments, sown by our own blindness, faithlessness, and fanaticism. This is not the language of an alarmist; it is prompted by the contemplation of our proceedings in India, and by authentic information from the natives themselves of the sentiments which they entertain; it is the language also of five out of six of the Company's servants, who have recently returned from India—of men who have used the opportunities which they enjoyed of observing the signs of the times; it is the language of all who are capable of connecting causes and consequences, and who know that insidiousness begets suspicion, and that intolerance engenders hate."

November 29th.—" What is now to be done? Shall we proceed onward and secure the key of India, or leave our frontiers exposed to the designs which have been so unequivocally developed during the present year, and which the prophetic genius of Napoleon predicted twenty-five years ago? It is clear beyond a doubt that after the demonstrations which have been made this year in Central Asia, our possessions are not safe while the passes of Cabul are in possession of a power whose hostility has been unreservedly manifested towards us.

"The course of political intrigue, of which Herat'h was only the index, seems to force upon us *the policy of still moving forward* if we would not shrink back to the limits of a factory."

December 20th.—" The Jami Jehan Noma is a native paper, taken in by most of the native chiefs of India. It is frequently full of treasonable remarks. In the number for November 4th, 1838, it was mentioned that ' The Mussulmen of Cabul had assembled to the number of 400,000 and were about to invade Hindostan, and that the English army destined for the conquest of Cabul had been assembled at Loodiana, and would march in a few days. The resident of Dehly was further reported in this paper to have remitted the tribute due from several rajahs, and to have got them to sign several new articles by way of treaty.'

" When the rajah heard this he observed, that the English gentlemen must be in great alarm and trepidation at the overwhelming numbers of the Shah of Cabul, since it has come to this pass that they were now remitting their claims of annual tribute, and entering into new treaties. Some of the people in the city and elsewhere observed, that the people of Hindoosthan were ever given to oppose established authority; and if the *Jami Jehan Noma*, which was taken in by most chiefs of Hindoosthan should give such versions of the force and people of Cabul, and of the expedition to that place, the chiefs of Hindoosthan and its ignorant people would, on hearing such exaggerated statements, *feel still more inclined to withdraw from their allegiance* and former contracts," &c. &c.

March 14th, 1839.—" A Persian army laid siege to Herat'h with the avowed intention of marching into India, and *the approach of Russian influence*, like that of a portentous comet, *began to disturb all the relations of our Indian empire.*"

Blackwood's Magazine, Dec. 1838.—" We have reduced the European force which in 1827 was 33,000, to twenty-five regiments, mustering little more than 19,000 men, and the native army which, in the former year, was 260,000 to 155,000. All this we have done in the full knowledge of the truth, emphatically impressed upon our government by our greatest commanders in India, even at the moment of the most signal triumphs, that without an adequate proportion of European troops, which should never be less than a third or a fourth of that of the soldiers (native), it was impossible to expect success in India; and that our empire in the East, on the appearance of the first European power, would be seriously endangered. Forgetting that there can be no inherent loyalty in a black Mussulman, or Hindoo, to a white Christian and distant crown, we have done much to dissolve the firm bond of union that has hitherto held us together—that of permanent self-

[Margin note: Interesting — native administrative affect via reduced pension and payment of soldiers.]

interest. Influenced by a blind and false spirit of economy, the Indian government has successively reduced the allowances, retired pensions, and other advantages accruing to the officers, European and native, as well as privates of the native army, so that not only has the attachment of these actually in the ranks been seriously injured and weakened, but the disposition to enlist under British colours throughout the whole peninsula, been chilled and discouraged to a most alarming degree.

"The way in which it was all along foreseen Russia would act, would be, to go on step by step, consolidating her power by successive acquisitions, and taking care always to precede her legions by subsidiary treaties and alliances, which might enable her to march through all the intervening country as through her own dominions, and pour at last with an accumulating force on the northern provinces of Hindoost'han. It is in vain to say that it is impossible for the Russian troops to march down from Russia to India, when the British troops *are preparing to march from Delhi and Agra to Cabul and Candahar, a distance of two thousand miles.* When our troops arrive in those regions, they will have gone more than half way from Calcutta to the shores of the Caspian, from which the Russian troops have to set out. They are setting out avowedly to anticipate the Russians in the possession of Cabul, and in all probability to assist the Shah of Herat'h in his resistance to the Russian guile and Persian forces."

Tuesday, May 2d, 1839.—" There can be no doubt that the dangers which have called the army of the Indus into the field are altogether without precedent since we first planted our standard in India. On every previous occasion our difficulties arose from combinations within the Indus; at the present crisis we are threatened with invasion by a conjunction of powers beyond that river, organized by a great European power of vast resources. Emissaries have been diligently employed through the length and breadth of Hindoostan, in sowing the seeds of disaffection among our own subjects, in rousing to hostility the minds of our subordinate allies, and in turning the eyes of India to the grand expedition as coming down from the west to put an end to our empire. These circumstances of unexampled difficulty called for instantaneous action, and for the adoption of a new and original plan of policy," &c. &c.

"If the dangers which threatened the empire had been imaginary, if they had even been exaggerated, there might have been some ground for censuring an expedition which involved us in the web of Avghan politics. *But the dangers were palpable and imminent,*" &c. " Russia would have been on the banks of the Indus with all the rabble of Western Asia at her heels. The Seiks, already endowed with a military education rather advanced, are too powerful to agree to their becoming docile instruments to the East India Company; and the proof of the spirit that animates them is the news recently brought, that the passage of the Panjab has been refused to the English. The alliance of the English with the aged Maha Rajah, can only be looked on as a forced alliance, destined to be broken as soon as a rupture can take place without compromising the safety of the empire of Runjeet'h Singh. In the interior of India the English have before them none but a hostile population, which support with impatience a foreign yoke: the people have gained nothing by the English occupation of the country. National industry has been completely ruined; the inferior classes are impoverished by the effort of the English, whose machinery excludes all competition," &c.—Augsburg Gazette of 24th of January.

July 11.—" When the accredited agent of Russia was at our gates, and the most vaunting reports were industriously spread that the hordes of Central Asia were marshalled by Russia, and were about to pour down on the plains of India, and when these boasts had begun materially to shake the confidence of the subsidiary chiefs throughout India, it was time to make some demonstration."

July 18.—" If any doubt had ever been entertained of the ambitious projects of Russia, in reference to the East, they must be at once dispelled by a perusal of the last note of that court. In it Russia assumes to have an equal interest with England in the affairs of Avghanistaun; after having herself so far interfered with this state, lying at so great a distance from her frontier, as to guarantee the transfer of Herath to the Kandahar chiefs, calls upon England to avoid all interference with it, though it lies upon our border; and its emissaries have endeavoured to spread disaffection through our empire. We can all remember the electrical effect produced on all minds and all interests by the raising of the siege, and the retirement of the Persian army. The funds rose four per cent! The march to Cabul appears now to have been a measure indispensably necessary to the security of the British empire in the East."

October 31st.—*The Kurnoul Conspiracy.*—" The capture of Kurnoul has brought to light a conspiracy against the British government which may well fill the mind with astonishment. Kurnoul is a state under the Madras Presidency, of small dimensions and limited revenues, the only remaining independent Mahomedan principality in the south. In consequence of information of treasonable preparations, the British troops were sent; the fort was occupied without opposition, and presented nothing beyond the ordinary means of defence. Upon more minute investigation, however, the zennanah or female apartments, were found to contain between four and five hundred pieces of ordnance, chiefly of brass, some concealed under ground, others immured in walled-up chambers, together with whatever was necessary for the most extensive military operations. One hundred pieces of ordnance were mounted and ready for action. Some of them had been cast in forms of surpassing beauty and exactness. The zennanah likewise contained many furnaces, some of which had been recently worked. All their preparations, so far beyond the resources of this petty state, and the intellect of its chief, manifest unequivocally a wide-spread conspiracy to annihilate the British authority in the south. In the silence and secrecy of the zennanah, shielded from intrusion by the inviolability of its character, have the dark designs of this combination been carried forward. The cannon, according to the description given, must have been cast under European superintendence. The expenses of these warlike preparations must have been furnished by more powerful agents; the contrivance and execution of this vast plan, in impenetrable obscurity, though under the very eye of government, must have been managed by wiser heads and deeper politicians than the foolish rajah, who is now a prisoner to his own troops, through having suffered their allowances to run into arrears. It is for government to unravel the ramifications, and trace the origin of a plot, which would probably have been consummated as soon as the Madras Presidency had been deprived of its strength by the despatch of an army to the Birmese empire.

"The discoveries have been almost exclusively confined to the nawaub's zennanah, which proves to be a perfect arsenal on a most extended scale; and you will stare to read that there have been found concealed in various ways, underground and in godowns whose doors and entrances had been built up, between four and five hundred pieces of artillery, of which fully one hundred are in such a state of equipment as to be ready for active service in the field at a few days' warning, &c. &c. &c. When we consider that this really gigantic magazine, from which the implements for the destruction of our empire were to have sprung, has been collecting and increasing daily in strength and extent, almost in the very heart of our dominions, in a manner so stealthy as to have been scarcely suspected by the government and their authorities, we are lost in astonishment at the extent and power of the resources which have furnished the means to dig so tremendous a mine beneath our feet, and in wonder and conjecture as to the time and the agents to be chosen or created for its explosion, &c. It only required the hand to the plough to burst with astounding fury over southern India."*

---

* The Kurnoul Rajah, when under the surveillance of the British government, was stabbed to death by one of his own followers whilst in attendance at an English church. There was a report that he intended to become a Christian, which was the pretext of his murder, although a well-founded suspicion exists that he was murdered to prevent disclosures.

Extract from the debate in the House of Commons on the motion for a vote of thanks to the army of the Indus.

Mr. Macaulay.—" During his residence in India frequent opportunities were presented to him of seeing evidence of the restless and unquiet feeling which prevailed, not only amongst our own subjects, not only amongst the subjects of neighbouring states, but amongst the people under the dominion of our subsidiary allies. In every quarter, in Nepaul, in Ava" (and Lahore), " change was contemplated with confident expectation, he may say by some anticipated with earnest hope. Military stores were collected, defences were raised, resources and treasures were husbanded, and in every direction a feeling was excited which must have terminated in the greatest calamities, were it not for the results which attended the wise government of Lord Auckland, and the brilliant achievements of the army under Lord Keane. He fully believed that had it not been for the triumphant consequences of the late campaign—accomplished as its triumphs were with a rapidity of which no previous example could be found,—he believed that had it not been for the valour, skill, and foresight of the officers, and for the unequalled bravery of the troops under their command, the security of our Indian possessions would have been very seriously impaired. Keeping these considerations in view, and assuming them to be facts beyond the possibility of question, he must be permitted to say that, however great might be the number of camp followers, however vast the supply of camels which attended the march of the army, the right honourable baronet opposite would not think the expense useless when he recollected the advantages which it had procured.—February 6th, 1840."—The expense here alluded to, I have understood from the mouth of Sir Alexander Burnes, the second functionary at Cabul in the civil employment of the Indian government, to have been, up to the period of the Shah Shujah ul Moolk's entrance into Cabul on the 7th of August 1839, two crores and a half of rupees, (two millions five hundred thousand pounds sterling.) The number of camels accompanying the army was, on the same authority thirty-five thousand head. It appears the whole number of souls comprised in the expedition when the army arrived at Quetta (Shawl and Musting,) amounted to eighty thousand.* The unquestionable dangers referred to by Mr. Macauley, it will be observed were and are of a local nature exclusively. How will these dangers be increased; to what certainty will they be reduced by the belligerent attitude of a great foreign power, a power sufficient of itself to contend with and subdue the resources of the Indian empire, though united and concentrated, and not, as Mr. Macauley observes, "restless and unquiet, anticipating and expecting with earnest hope, a change of rulers!"

* Calcutta journals, official returns.

CHAPTER VII.

DESCRIPTIVE CHARACTER OF DOST MAHOMED EX-AMEER OF CABUL.

THE Ameer Dost Mahomed, son of Sir Uffraz, Paienda Khan Barikzye, is of high descent amongst the Avghans, and claims a natural equality with the tribe of Suddoozye, from which the Dooraunee king is selected. But this circumstance of royal precedence gives the Suddoozye tribe a political superiority. I believe he was born near Djillalabad, although I have heard his nativity ascribed to Kandhar, in 1793. By an honorary or devotional vow of his mother he was consecrated to the lowest menial service of the sacred cenotaph of Lamech, a place of sanctity for the resort of pious Mahomedans near Djillalabad (or Ningrahar). This cenotaph is known in the colloquial dialect of the country by the appellation of Meiter Lam. In conformity with the maternal vow, when the young aspirant became capable of wielding a brush, he was carried to Meiter Lam by his mother, and instructed to exonerate her from the consequences of a sacred obligation, by sweeping, for the period of a whole day, the votive area included within the precincts of the holy space enclosing the alleged tomb of the antediluvian, the father, as he is termed, of the prophet Noah! Very little attention was paid in early life to develope the natural faculties of his mind by artificial means. He was the protegé of experience and necessity, and those impartial and inexorable tutors were the constant mentors of this child, as they are of all who successfully *climb* the ladder of ambition. His mother was of the Kizzlebashe tribe, which forms the mercenary imperial guard of Persian origin. They are similar to the late janissaries of Turkey, and though denominated slaves, were of prætorian dignity and power; they are also called "Jowan share," which is the Persian for "young lion," and has the same signification as "Yeugi cherri," the Toorkey for "janissary."

Amongst the descendants of the high-born ladies of the Dooraunee race he was subject to be slighted; and he, together with an elder brother labouring under similar natal inferiority, were excluded by the more fortunate brethren as an ignoble scion of paternal liaison. The father of Dost Mahomed had twenty-one sons, all of whom grew up to man's estate, and were individuals of character, property, and influence. Dost Mahomed very early in life chose the profession of a soldier, or rather the idleness consequent on the disqualifications of birth gave him full leisure to indulge the tendency of his genius, and he attached himself, in the character of pesh khidmut, or personal attendant, to his eldest brother, the Vizier Futty Khan. The versatile and romantic history of this chivalric warrior afforded his young attendant frequent opportunities of distinguishing himself; and an act of deliberate murder, when about fourteen years of age, was the first circumstance which attracted the vizier's attention towards him, and pointed him out as a man of bold and daring enterprise.

The vizier, annoyed, disgusted, and perhaps intimidated by the proximity of an enemy, expressed a wish inimical to his personal safety in the presence of Dost Mahomed, about the time of leaving his public levee. The obnoxious individual, at the moment the young man egressed from the durbar, unwittingly passed on horseback. Our young soldier was also *en cavalier*, and armed with a rifle. They came face to face in the public street of Peshour, and in a moment the youth shot his brother's enemy, in the midst of a numerous body of clansmen. He fled to the vizier with the news, assuring him of the death of his rival. The protection of his brother, who then possessed the uncontrolled ministerial power under the confiding and voluptuous Shah Mahmoud, and exercised paramount authority over the Avghan tribes, was sufficient to shield him from the consequences of the "lex talionis," and guaranteed an immunity against that vindictive passion which is so eminently characteristic of the Avghan race.

The adventurous life of a Khorassannee cavalier early opened the way to his acquisition of the essential qualifications for a military leader, and his capacious mind and tractability of temper rewarded the anxious anticipations of maternal care with the alluring prospect of future political supremacy. At the age of sixteen he was eminent for personal bravery, recklessness, and the juvenile and martial accomplishments of a good horseman, a fair shot with the rifle, and an expert spearsman in the national equestrian exercise of the "Ishpillak." Previous to the sanguinary service alluded to above, he was a neglected attaché at the levee of his elder brother; and there are still some reminiscences which represent his moral character at that youthful period in an unfavourable light. To those acquainted with the vicious habits of Nawaub Semmund Khan (another brother of Dost Mahomed, many years older than himself), it may only be necessary to say, that the young aspirant was some time amongst the most beautiful of all the juvenile attendants who were a disgrace to the domestic establishment of that licentious devotee of Avghan debauchery: so little was his fraternity regarded by the highborn sons of Sir Affraz Khan. After that exertion of a determined spirit, which pleaded for the vizier's personal favour, he was no longer found amongst the forlorn " deliciæ" at the indiscriminating orgies of the sensual and unfraternal Nawaub. He was employed by the vizier to settle the affairs of the Kohdamun at an early age, and the government of that insubordinate and treacherous part of the Avghan population was entrusted to him, whose recklessness gave assurance of success, where a bloody system of private revenge, indulged with quickness, avidity, and asperity, had become incorporated with the habits of an irascible and capricious people. He played with them at their own game, upon what would now be considered the homœopathic plan, and in the end attained a character for perfidy not surpassed by any Avghan within our notice, and quite equal to the most despotic vagaries of the ancient Persian princes. All the refractory chiefs of the Kohistaun, (the remote mountainous district within the jurisdiction of the city of Cabul, or metropolitan vicinage,) were one after another destroyed by encouraging internal warfare. Their family feuds were exasperated, and the system of revenge was carried out to an awful extent—often to the extermination of all the objects of jealousy which wealth, respectability, or political power brought within the discriminating view of a rapacious eye. In short, Dost Mahomed, when a mere boy, gained the reputation of an expert diplomatist amongst the Avghans; a character which Machiavel might have studied with the certainty of *scientific* improvement!

With the Ameer the end justified the means. His political enemies were made the victims of confidence—inveigled into his power by a series of sacred asseverations, and their lives extinguished without reluctance or compunction.

On the death of Mahomed Azeem Khan, the full brother of Vizier Futty Khan, who had been previously literally chopped to pieces alive, limb by limb, by order of Kameran Mirza, the son of Mahmood Shah, the sovereignity of Cabul fell into the hereditary possession of Hubeeb Ullah Khan, Mahomed Azeem's eldest son. His barbarity and recklessness soon induced the chiefs of the country to turn their attention towards Dost Mahomed as a more manageable leader than Hubeeb Ullah. His debauchery and dissolute life presented him to their view as an individual who would readily receive the dictation of their order; and he was called to the paramount power of government by the unanimous voice of all the feudal lords, supported by the popular voice of the citizens of Cabul, which capital always exercised a great metropolitan influence in the general politics of the country at large. The day Dost Mahomed ascended the Musnud he performed the "Toba," which is a solemn and sacred formula of reformation, in reference to any accustomed moral crime or depravity of habit. He was followed in the Toba by all his chiefs, who found themselves obliged to keep pace with the march of mind—to prepare for the defensive system of policy this assumption of purity on the part of the prince suggested. The Toba was a sort of declaration of principles; and the chiefs viewing it in that light, beheld their hopes of supremacy in imminent hazard. Thus a subject of jealousy, and the germ of dissolution, inherent even in the most perfect forms of government, were here implanted at the constitution of the oligarchy. Many years subsequent to this period, when Dost Mahomed introduced the European discipline into a part of his army, the measure was suggested by the ambition to relieve himself from the irksomeness of surveillance,—the suspicions of his chiefs were confirmed, their motives to resistance determined; and the necessity of self-defence dictated a coalition with the King Shujah Ul Moolk and his English co-operatives, when they invaded Avghanistaun.

In later life the Ameer became sensible of the advantages arising from learning. Although knowledge of literature amongst Mahomedan nations is confined to a contracted sphere, at least the reputation of theological science was essential to the chief upon whom had been conferred the title of Ameer Ul Momineen, or commander of the faithful. To escape the humility of dependence upon subordinate agents, more especially the secretaries necessarily employed in all revenue and judicial transactions, he tasked his mind with the acquisition of letters, and became worthy, by his industry and success in the pursuit, of the respect of the great, as he commanded the admiration of the vulgar, who are ever accustomed to venerate the divinity of wisdom.

In 1833 Shah Shujah, who had been thirty years an exile, during the greater part of which period he resided at Loodiannah, and was a stipendiary of the British government, attempted the recovery of his throne. His majesty concentrated his forces at Kandhar. Dost Mahomed advanced from Cabul to raise the siege of that metropolis, in which design he succeeded in the spring of 1834. The king was defeated, and the chiefs of Cabul insisted upon the measure of constituting their prince " Ameer," and his highness consequently was wrought up to the ambition of an alluring title, that exalted him conspicuously above his contemporaries and coadjutors; and the commemoration of victory by the ascent of dignity covered the object of its consecration with the mantle of glory.

The title of Ameer is simply political; but as politics always forms a part of the religion of Mahomedans, the prince's flatterers soon added to the semi-royal distinction "Ul Momineen," and he became, in colloquial acceptation, " commander of the faithful," as they euphoniously style the Khulleefa or Calif of the Mahomedan world. The coin of Cabul, which, since the change of dynasty had been struck in the name of " Saheb i Zeman," which is incognito or *innominally* " ruler of the day or the time then passing," was now impressed with the cognizance of " Ameer Dost Mahomed, by the grace of God." The word " ghazee, or fighter of the faith," was also added, which is the enviable and ever-desirable cognomen of Mahomedan princes, as the most acceptable passport to apotheosis.

Simultaneously with the battle of Kandhar, Runjeet'h Singh, Prince of the Panjab, crossed the Indus with designs of conquest, and seized on Peshour, which is one of the capital cities of Avghanistaun.

To remain at rest and apparently unmolested by a conquest of the Seiks encroaching so fearfully upon his natural territory, although the jurisdiction of Peshour had been under the government of a brother who acknowledged no control, was unbecoming the character of the Ameer; and the pretext of a religious war, which is at any time capable of bringing around the Prince's standard swarms and hordes of religious fanatics, enthusiasts and bigots, was promulgated against Runjeet'h and his infidel Seiks; and the Ameer ul Momineen appeared on the plain of Peshour with fifty thousand belligerent candidates for martyrdom and immortality. Savages from the remotest recesses of the mountainous districts, who were dignified with the profession of the Mahomedan faith, many of them giants in form and strength, promiscuously armed with sword and shield, bows and arrows, matchlocks, rifles, spears, and blunderbusses, concentrated themselves around the standard of religion, and were prepared to slay, plunder, and destroy for the sake of God and the Prophet, the unenlightened infidels of the Panjab. In this expedition the Ameer was not attended with success: the diplomacy of his rival* made him withdraw

---

* On the occasion of Dost Mahomed's visit to Peshour, which occurred during the period of my service with Runjeet'h Singh, I was despatched by this Prince as ambassador to the Ameer. I divided his brothers against him, exciting their jealousy of his growing power, and exasperating the family feuds, with which from my previous acquaintance I was familiar, and stirred up the feudal

without a battle; and retreating to Cabul he resumed, until another opportunity should occur, the pacific administration of his government. But the assumption of the title of Ameer ul Momineen pledged him to a system of perpetual hostility with the infidels in his vicinity, although the ambitious tendency of that aggressive position was not sustained by the acquisition of additional resources for the maintenance of his new pretensions.

The Ameer pursued his literary labours, and completed the task of reading the Koran after two years' application, familiarizing his efforts by a repetition of his toil until the performance had been twice accomplished. By this means he acquired a knowledge of letters that enabled him to give his personal attention to some of the most important addresses and petitions occasionally preferred by the necessitous, and was freed in a great measure from the strict tutelage of the Kizzlebashe chiefs, represented at his court by the Mirzas, who were all to a man of that persuasion, and constituted by

---

lords of his durbar, with the prospect of pecuniary advantages. I induced his brother, Sooltaun Mahomed Khan, the lately deposed chief of Peshour, with 10,000 retainers, to withdraw suddenly from his camp about nightfall. The chief accompanied me towards the Seik camp, whilst his followers fled to their mountain fastnesses. So large a body retiring from the Ameer's control in opposition to his will, and without previous intimation, threw the general camp into inextricable confusion, which terminated in the clandestine rout of his forces, without beat of drum, or sound of bugle or the trumpet's blast, in the quiet stillness of midnight. At daybreak no vestige of the Avghan camp was seen, where, six hours before, 50,000 men and 10,000 horses, with all the busy host of attendants, were rife with the tumult of wild commotion. An elaborate account of this diplomatic mission from the Prince of the Panjab to the Ameer of Cabul, will be minutely related in my forthcoming personal journal.

their "esprit de corps" a formidable phalanx amongst the functionaries of the Ameer's durbar.

The Ameer is now forty-nine years of age and in vigorous health. When he stands erect his height is six feet, but there is a slight stoop in the neck arising from a rounded contour of the shoulders, characteristic of his family, which militates against the commanding appearance his person is otherwise formed to impress when animated by conversation or excited by passion. He has large features and a muscular frame; a heavy tread in his walk, placing the sole of his foot all at once flat upon the ground, which indicates that the instep is not well arched. The outline of his face is Roman. Having a curved jaw, a low retreating forehead, hair of the head shaven, and the turban worn far back, gives an appearance of elevation to the frontal region, although the facial angle is scarcely less acute than in some of the higher orders of *simiæ*. The nose is aquiline, high, and rather long, and finished with beautiful delicacy; the brow open, arched, and pencilled; the eyes are hazel-gray, not large, and of an elephantine expression; the mouth large and vulgar and full of bad teeth; the lips moderately thick; ears large. The shape of the face is oval, rather broad across the cheeks, and the chin covered with a full strong beard, originally black, now mixed with gray hairs. This appendage is dyed once a week, that is, on Thursday morning, in the process of general ablution in the hummaum or warm bath. To this usage all respectable Mahomedans are accustomed preparatory to the seventh day's appropriation of a period for public worship, which is Friday, commencing with Thursday at 12 o'clock and terminating at the last prayer on Friday evening, or to 12 o'clock at night. His dress is unaffected and plain, being made of various materials, in conformity with the season. The kubbah or frock, is, according to the Persian fashion, cut low before the breast to display the p'heron or shirt, which is usually of red or crimson silk from Heraut'h. The choga (or toga) he wore was a large flowing robe, with very capacious sleeves tightened at the wrists. In summer the material of the under dress is white longcloth, bordered along the margins on the inner side with a stripe two inches deep of flowered chintz, manufactured in Cabul. The choga of a sprig pattern, or pine-flowered European chintz, English or German. In winter he wore silk, commonly satin, lightly wadded and closely quilted; colour, green or yellow. The sleeves of the kubbah are provided with loops, and may be opened or closed along the lower seam as far as the elbow from the wrists, and fit tight to the arm when the loops are laced. When open they hang like a long piece of drapery from the elbow. The seams are all run with gold cord, about the calibre of a crowquill; gold lace, an inch broad, decorates the edges of the open breast; and the shoulders and middle of the arms, and the back between the shoulders, are embellished with gold embroidery in floral devices. The choga in winter is made of English broadcloth; olive brown was a favourite colour; the seams braided with silk cord, and the edges run with an extremely narrow tape, all of the same sombre hue as the garment; and it was also decorated with embroidery similar to the kubbah, but in silk cord. When the weather becomes severe, every one who can afford the expense throws over all a large lambskin cloak, the wool on which is worn inside. The material resembles our finest doeskin. The wealthy have them exquisitely wrought in green or yellow floss silk, representing the superb embroidery on Cashmere shawls. For the poor they are plain, and when the cloak is made of sheepskin it is very cheap. The pantaloons or drawers are capacious, and made of longcloth, or striped red and white silk called *dirre-eye*. The stockings were white or blue spotted, quite fine, and knit in Cabul. Shoes, usually red leather and plain; sometimes those of India were worn, which are ornamented with spangles, and embroidered with gold thread. The turban consisted in summer of a piece of English sprigged or plain fine light white muslin, twelve yards long and a yard wide, and a cashmere shawl in winter. The loins were girt with a duplicate of the headdress, folded tight over the kubbah; and the fancy occasionally indulged in a loongee, of Peshour manufacture, with gold ends. This is a kind of material peculiar to the place of its construction. It is made of cotton, and the pattern resembles exactly our common check, but is finely made, and may be valued, when ornamented with deep gold ends, at seventy or eighty rupees. It is formed of two pieces sewn down the middle, each three yards long and half a yard broad.

The Ameer's manners were those of an educated Asiatic, and the fact is most remarkable, that all this family possess the "shirrum i huzzoor" in an eminent degree; that is, extreme modesty, approaching to diffidence, which renders him incapable of denying a favour in the presence of the individual who prefers a suit with delicacy and tact! In conversation he is boisterous and energetic, which are habits arising from the military life he has been accustomed to; extremely susceptible to flattery, beyond measure vain, and fond of pleasantry. He is inattentive to forms, but jealous of all the respect that the strictest etiquette could demand. He is a monster of rapacity; this quality is a natural vice with him; his eyes had a feline glare when he looked full in the face of any one, and they assumed an awakened stare of attention when the accumulation of gold was the subject of his thoughts. As a politician he knew well the character of every class of the population, having himself had practical experience of the whole range of human society, in all the forms in which the social bodies of that country present themselves to observation. He was accustomed to employ policy in ordinary intercourse with society, although the most revolting cruelty was recklessly practised on all occasions of exacting money. He is extremely vain of his talents as a speaker, and will sometimes declaim at great length, and with a good deal of eloquence, on trivial subjects. In these pretensions he was indulged by his flatterers, who listened with attention, and assented to his arguments with frequent exclamations of admiration. He is loud and vociferous on most occasions, as he seems to be always excited. When menaced by events of a grave, solemn, and important character, he becomes dignified, quiet, submissive, and, if the affair should take a hopeless turn, he timidly and readily listens to the advice of any one, not even excepting his personal domestics; and they are ever ready to display their influence by gratuitous interference. When the Ameer gave way to a desponding tone of mind, which was frequently the case, his perfidious principles caused him to mistrust every body, and he is consequently without a friend. On great emergencies he becomes fearful and apprehensive, and sometimes loses his presence of mind. When the wife of Suddoo Khan, the Ameer's sister, suborned one of my soldiers to murder her husband, information was conveyed to his highness at two o'clock, A. M. Relating the event to me next day he said, "I began to be alarmed, at that dead hour of the night, in the midst of my haram, and calling for my dagger, placed it under my pillow." I replied, that he did well, for it would have been heavy odds against him if such a host as formed the domestic establishment about his highness was to become insubordinate in the solitude of night. Approaching his horse to mount, with the prospect of battle before him, he has been known to put the wrong foot in the stirrup, which, had he finished the intention, would have placed his face towards the animal's tail! This occurred when he was encamped near Peshour. Runjeet'h's forces occupied the plain, and the Ameer determined to offer battle in opposition to his council of state. Confused and bewildered with the fearful results to be apprehended, more from conflicting councils than the weapons of the foe, he resisted not the kindness of a friend, who gently solicited him to reconsider his last resolve!

The Ameer in early life, and until the age of thirty, was addicted to drunkenness. During his fits of intoxication, many ruthless acts of indiscriminate barbarity were the result of these depraved hallucinations. Surrounded by a crowd of drunken revellers, maddened by the maniac draught of the frantic bowl, friend and colleague, master, man, and slave, all indiscriminate and promiscuous actors in the wild, voluptuous, licentious scene of shameless bacchanals, they caroused and drank with prostitutes, and singers, and fiddlers, day and night, in one long, interminable cycle,—the libertine's eternity of sensual excitement and continuous debauchery; and this tenor of life was encouraged by his retainers, who admired in his heedless vices the unrestrained license of feudal supremacy.

It is related that when Dost Mahomed was a wanderer in the fastnesses about Ghiznee, that fortress and vicinity being in his possession, a valuable caravan, in transit from Bocharah to India, encamped for the night under the walls of the citadel. The followers of the predatory chief were unanimous in recommending him to *borrow* a large sum of money from the travelling merchants. They all sallied out armed in the train of their chief, with the design of making friends with the caravan. On the road Dost Mahomed suddenly drew up his charger, and exclaimed, " Brothers, what are we going to do? God knows whether these poor merchants will ever receive payment of the gold we take from them—*as a loan*—which we agreed among ourselves to solicit. And what are we to do with the money after we get it? Shall we buy dominion with the plunder of the unfortunate? God forbid! Victory is of God, and he conferreth glory and power upon those whom he will cherish. No! it is better that we pass by this temptation of the devil, and see what Heaven has in reserve for us, ' for patience, though a bitter plant, produces sweet fruit.' " And so he returned upon his steps, and the hour of the day favouring the indulgence of leisure, he alighted on an eminence near the road, which afforded him a prospect of the route towards Cabul. At this moment a messenger appeared from the city with an invitation from the Kizzlebashe leaders of his opponent, pressing him to the assumption of the government, which their treason to the incumbent placed at his command. He immediately uncovered his head, and in the posture of supplication repeated the *Fatteah* or initial prayer, which is an invocation and religious formula in use among Mahomedans, and precedes the beginning of every important enterprise. He added, " God is great! Behold, how dominion is the gift of God! Blessed be the light of immortality!—Mount, and away for Cabul!"

The acquisition of sovereignty presented the prince in the character of a sincere reformer, in which effort of morals he was imitated by his court with truth and unmeasured pertinacity. In youth he was bold from necessity, but probably the experience of years, and the voluptuous excesses of luxurious leisure, in taking off the wiry edge from the sword of his ambition, dulled the instrument, and depraved its temper. I believe he is naturally timid, and I am unable to instance an example of his highness ever having boldly risked his person in an individual conflict. At the battle of Kandhar he and Shujah simultaneously ran away from each other. Dost Mahomed was the first to hear of his antagonist's flight. When satisfied that the field was entirely clear of the enemy, he rallied with becoming fierceness. " Stand!" cried his mentor, " where would the houseless and the hopeless flee? The ground thou standest upon is all the world to thee! the victor's throne or grave of victory! Stand for God and the Prophet, (on whom be eternal peace,) and thy own dear self. 'Tis paradise in death—in triumph, royalty!"

This cautious valour, which is characteristic of the Ameer, it is said by his followers has become more conspicuous since his reformation of dissolute habits removed the cloud of intemperate exuberance which envelopes the psychological phenomena of the military mind; or perhaps the sagacity of his judges has become more astute and captious by a system of abstinence, for " tee-totalism" was all the vogue amongst the courtiers of a reformed debauchee. Nevertheless, his perfect knowledge of the people over whom he was called to rule, and his unprincipled readiness at despotic sway, made him remarkably well adapted to govern the worse than savage tribes he had to command, especially when sustained by the powerful influence of the prætorian or janissary tribe of Kizzlebashe. He is no believer in human principle, but a self-convicted and unchanging doubter of every motive but self-interest, and is ever on the alert to seize by craftiness the object which any one possessing power would attempt by the direct exertion of optional authority. He is liable to frequent despondency, but is too politic to display this infirmity of feeling to common observation. It is only during a period of relaxation that he has been known to give way to the depression of mind. He is an exquisite dissembler so long as his affairs are subservient to his will; but the equanimity of his mind is liable to be deranged by untoward events, and on some occasions he has been known to shed unavailing tears of hopelessness, and fly for advice and consolation to the presence of his favourite wife, Khadija. To this lady he is superstitiously attached, and probably he has been indebted to her circumspection and humanity for all the greatness he attained. She is not less rapacious than the Ameer, but the general tenor of her mind and manners are amiably adapted to her situation and rank. I am convinced her masculine spirit sustained him to the last, and could he have been guided by her sagacious mind, his affairs would have taken a totally different turn in the result of the diplomatic intercourse with the Indian government. This lady, as the mother of his heir, for whom the succession was designed, was the sultanah of the haram, called, by the Toorks, Walidah or " Queen-Mother." The Ameer's fortitude and bravery are questionable, but he is gifted with a pertinacity of perseverance amounting to capricious obstinacy, and is a most relentless enemy; with him the principle of avarice was an active motive; gold was his god, and blood-feuds were reconciled, murders compounded for, justice swayed out of the sober path of duty, and the connivance of every abuse, civil, political, and moral, admitted in the observances of his devotion. There was nothing so good as not to be contemned—nothing was so bad as not to be honoured; every design, however vile, was sterling merit when proposed with a bribe. Had his pretensions been sustained by principles of virtue, his manners would have entitled him to the appellation and dignity of a highly refined man; but he is known to be impure in his domestic habits. He indulges to excess in the lascivious sensualities so fascinating to the Oriental imagination, and consistent with the beatitude of their paradise. In the pursuit of these forbidden liaisons, impulse putting to flight the dignity of propriety, he has not unfrequently subjected himself to singular and grotesque positions, although the certain consequence of such infidelity would be a severe and voluble castigation, followed by an irksome coolness of manner on the part of the sultanah, which endured until domestic harmony should be restored by the incidents of reconciliation constantly recurring in matrimonial communion, when strife is not the fruit of a discrepancy in temper or a consequence of deficient affection. He revelled and luxuriated in voluptuous and unrestrained licentiousness.

His family consists of several wives and numerous descendants, with an endless train of slaves and other domestic attendants. Khadija, his principal wife, and sultanah of his haram, is a noble Dooraunee lady of the Populzye tribe. She has a sister in the haram of Shujah ul Moolk. She is the mother of the most esteemed progeny of his highness. Her offspring are five sons and a daughter. The eldest son is Mahomed Akber Khan, lately become notorious to the world by his exploits in the recent massacre of the British army and death of their distinguished political chief. This young prince is the heir apparent of the Ameer, and has attained great reputation for bravery in the Avghan religious wars with the Seiks. He commanded the army sent by the Ameer at my suggestion against the Seik force of Peshour in the spring of 1837. A battle was fought at Jemrood in which two thousand Seiks, with Herree Singh, Runjeet'h's commander-in-chief, were killed, and also a thousand Avghans. Second, Hyder Khan, who was taken prisoner by the English on the fall of Ghiznee, where this young prince commanded. Third, Share Jan. Fourth, Mahomed, Ameen. Fifth, Mahomed—(name not recollected).

The eldest is twenty-five years of age, and the youngest past seven. The daughter is married to a son of Mahomed Abzeem Khan's, and the two eldest sons are also wedded to their cousin-germans, both having two wives each, one of whom, in the case of Mahomed Akber, is of an inferior Avghan tribe, and consequently no relation. He married her, to whom he had been long betrothed, when himself and family retreated into Tatary as the British army advanced upon Cabul. The Ameer's oldest son, Mahomed Ufzell Khan, is twenty-seven years of age; he lost his mother at an early period, a misfortune which has kept him back in life. His mother was of the Kizzlebashe tribe, and he is supposed to be biased in his sectarian principles towards the creed of the Persian schism. He was esteemed the head of the Kizzlebashe faction, whose interests he always sustained. He has a brother the exact image of his father, named Mahomed Azim. This young man, now in his twenty-third year, lost his moral reputation in a debauch with a Persian adventurer when on foreign service not long since, away from the influence of paternal control, and is now suffered to stand disregarded at the lower end of the Durbar, amongst the inferior subordinates of the government attachés. when he appears to pay his respects at the morning levees. Khadije, (the diminutive of Khadija), from her experience and influence as the mother of his heir, exercises paramount power in the haram, and is in fact the ruler's queen; but the lady who from rank and birth is entitled to that appellation, is Aga Taj. This lady has the misfortune to be placed in a position peculiarly painful. The daughter of Shah

Zada Abbass, Shujah's half brother by a Persian lady, she is a princess royal of the ancient regime, the grandchild of Timour Shah. Her father, who was some time King of Cabul, fled to Lahore, and deserted his family, most of whom remained at the capital. Aga Taja was forcibly seized by Dost Mahomed, and she became his lawful wife, but her high blood even now, although she has several children, will never let her speak of the Ameer by any other title than " Dosoo," a familiar nickname which the great apply to their slaves who may chance to have the cognomen of " Dost." She vaunts her princely origin, and calls the father of her children " her slave." Her person is quite diminutive, but a perfect beau ideal of exquisite and fairy-like perfection. It has been said she wore a luscious black mustache—a fine pencilled line upon the upper lip—but this assertion is an error; her beauty claims no propinquity of the kind with a trait so masculine. Her eldest child is a daughter; the next a son nine years old, called after his mother's great grandfather Ahmed Shah, the founder of the Suddoozye dynasty. Third, a son, Mahomed Zeman, in his seventh year. Fourth, fifth, and sixth, three daughters, the eldest of whom has just entered her sixth year, and the youngest was born in the fall of 1838. Her first-born was affianced to the second son of Nawaub Jubbar Khan, the Ameer's eldest surviving brother, and their nuptials were celebrated at Tash Khoorghaun, the capital of Khoolum, when they reached that city in their flight into Tatary. Whether victory should attend on the banner of her lord, or whether her uncle Shujah ascended the throne, Aga Taj was still the sufferer. The first event obscured the glory of her royal house, the second inflicted domestic misfortune. Her eldest son has a right royal presence, and her highness is herself a lady of princely bearing. Her high birth commands respect even from the sultanah mother; but Aga Taj has not the talent to turn to political account the regard of her husband, or the submissive veneration which birth commands from those of inferior degree. Frequent ebullitions of ill feeling are faintly suppressed betwixt the princess born, and the princess elect, the mother of Mahomed Akber.

When the English agent who visited Cabul in 1837-38, produced his presents for the Ameer's haram, (a breach of etiquette most inexcusable in any one pretending to a knowledge of Oriental customs,) they were distributed by the sultanah-mother, and it may be readily conceived that a more onerous duty could not have been imposed on her ladyship, although the value of these donations was inconsiderable, and adapted only to the frivolous tastes of savages, or the wretched fancies of rude infatuated Africans. They consisted of pins, needles, scissors, penknives, silk handkerchiefs, toys, watches, musical snuff-boxes, &c., all of which were received with inexpressible surprise, and the feeling followed by a sense of strong disgust, intermingled with mortification and disappointment. Anticipations a long time entertained, founded on the fact that Dost Mahomed had *conditionally* solicited the advent of a British agent at Cabul, and sustained by the Ameer's cupidity, kept their expectations alive with the hope of a golden subsidy. His highness was honoured with a pair of pistols and a spy-glass, as though the Governor-General would have suggested to the Ameer an allegory of the conservative and offensive symbols of good government! Dost Mahomed exclaimed with a "pish!" as he threw them down before him and averted his face—"Behold! I have feasted and honoured this Feringee to the extent of six thousand rupees, and have now a lot of pins and needles and sundry petty toys to show for my folly!" His humiliation was extreme. Every subterfuge that duplicity could devise, and every pretext that cunning could suggest, were used to work upon the English agent. The imaginary terrors of a Russian invasion were prominently displayed to him, and menaces of his personal safety were not spared to exact the ultimatum of his views, and prevail upon him to accede to the Ameer's designs. But all in vain is the wisdom of man to contend with the arm of fate! As a last effort one of the refractory brothers of the Ameer, who ruled in Kandhar, was solicited to visit Cabul, and propose at a final conference an ultimatum for the decision of the English agent. Assembled in general council they proposed the following questions and preamble.

"Mahomed Shah (the King of Persia) offers to the Avghans the acquisition of Heraut'h, and guarantees the permanency of their power by an offensive and defensive treaty with a subsidy of —— rupees; the treaty to be guaranteed by the Russian ambassador. Will the British government do this?"—Answer, No! From that moment the English agent was dismissed with immediate, and somewhat indecorous haste, though respectfully, and with presents of pacific propitiation, consisting of three or four horses, tolerably fair in value. Preparations for his departure from Cabul were immediately planned, the arrangements hurried with characteristic dread of delay, and large sums expended to insure the safe and speedy transport of the baggage belonging to the mission. The party leaving Cabul, proceeded with unusual despatch for travellers. Reaching Jillalabad, they threw themselves upon floats extemporaneously and instantly prepared, by which manœuvre they saved three days, and swept down the rapid current of the Cabul river, with apprehensions perturbed as the stream. Their fears were not unfounded. The Avghans were indignant at the result of the negotiations; and I have heard Dost Mahomed remark, " The greatest error of my life lay in this, that I allowed the English deceiver to escape with his head!" But this was at a later period—when the British army reached Kandhar— he added, " Fool that I was! God had given me a competency, and, dissatisfied with enough, I have ruined my affairs by making myself the pivot of foreign diplomacy; and in falling I meet the award due to the violation of duty, in disdaining the blessings of heaven."

The distribution of the English trifles almost caused an insurrection amongst the inmates of the haram. Aga Taj thought her children entitled to choose before all the others, but in this fancy her highness was not gratified, and the disappointment gave rise to many expressions of asperity against the ruling power in the haram. Her little boy got hold of a musical toy called an accordion. As a matter of course, he soon managed to put it out of order, and her highness supposing, in common with all Asiatics, that a Christian is capable of every science, sent it to me with a request to repair it. I regretted the task exceeded my abilities in mechanics. I learned from this source, the child of the princess royal, the ridicule and disgust which the English diplomacy and munificence excited in the minds of the ladies was general in the Ameer's family, and did more to lessen the agent's ascendancy at the court of Cabul than can easily be imagined by those who are unacquainted with the potency of backstair influence in an Oriental court.

Another of the Ameer's lawful wives is a lady of high rank, the widow of his highness's brother, Mahomed Azeem Khan, who succeeded the Vizier Futty Khan. She had two daughters by her first husband, who were married to two of Dost Mahomed's sons, so that the father married the mother and two of his sons married his wife's children—a strange confusion of relationship, that would puzzle a college of heralds to classify. He had some compunctions about forming the connexion, by the intermarriage of the offspring; but, as the lady possessed great wealth, it was expedient to marry her. He accordingly applied to the cazee, who instructed him to first give away the daughters to his sons, and afterwards marry the widow of his brother. He then plundered this lady of all her jewels, which were of great value. She had no offspring by the Ameer, and lived in the haram without note or influence. There was also a Highland lassie whom the Ameer married to strengthen his authority in the Kohistaun. She had a son, Akram Khan, now twenty-four years old. This is the young man who commanded (under my tutelage) the expedition into Tatary, of which my division formed a part, when a detachment of the Cabul army crossed the Caucasian range of mountains, in the war of 1838–39, against the Prince of Kundooz, Meer Muraad Beg. An Avghan of the Khoorum race, which is of the Sheah persuasion, occupying the remote valley near Bunnoo, was amongst the family of the Ameer. She had a son called Mahomed —— (name not recollected), about ten years old.—A prostitute, formerly in the service of Mahomed Azeem Khan, was married by the Ameer. She has given birth to two male children, the eldest six, and the other four years old. For these little ones he has great affection, and their mother is no less favoured than the most happy member of the Ameer's haram. Latterly, the Ameer married, in a quiet way, without any kind of ostentation, a daughter of Nusser Ullah Khan, some time treasurer of the Ameen ul Moolk, deceased. Her father was a refugee or emigrant at the court of Bocharah, to which place he fled to avoid the consequences of plebeian wealth, for in Cabul no parvenu, unless strongly sustained by the force of powerful patronage, could be tolerated in the possession of riches above his degree. The Ameer proposed to himself, by the marriage of the treasurer's daughter, to inveigle her father back to Cabul by the prospect of princely alliance; but the plan was amongst the few unsuccessful schemes of his highness, whose finesse occasionally surpassed itself! The Ameen ul Moolk mentioned above, left a widow of singular beauty and reputed wealth, and the Ameer, who is a constant admirer of these two rare qualities, took her into his haram as a wife; but they soon became mutually disgusted, and parted company by a friendly compact—the lady having been disburdened of her jewelled freight by the piracy of love! For the rest, his *liaisons* amongst the attendants of the haram, permanent and transient, were numerous and characteristic of unsagacious reason, of the non-instinctive *homo sapiens*, that is more promiscuous than the motiveless instigations of mere instinct, which neither changes the order of nature nor multiplies causes. For the subsistence of his haram, each female, who was dignified by the rank of a wife, had a specific allowance, out of which she maintained herself and domestic establishment. Matrimonial communion was occasionally sweetened, when such palliatives were recommended by the versatility of vagrant tastes, by sumptuous presents of Indian brocades, Cashmere shawls, jewels, and the less costly, though highly esteemed wonders of the European looms—chintzes, silks, and fine cottons. The children were kept in the haram and educated there; the females until the period of consummating an affianced bride, and the boys until they became old enough to bear arms or threaten to perform military duty. Those who had mothers to sustain their pretensions were prodigiously precocious, and the age of twelve years was not considered an immature period of life for the induction of a favourite protegé into the condition of incipient manhood. The neophyte is then allowed a separate establishment and a few military followers, and this courted distinction affords the young man the grateful opportunity of rewarding the fidelity of his early attached retainers, who hang on to the fate of their superior through all the changes that destiny can control, with her ever fitful and capricious mockery of human wisdom.

The Ameer occupied, with his family, a palace built by one of the Suddoozye kings. The Avghan chiefs under the oligarchy were no inconsistent advocates of disloyal politics. Suiting the action to the word, they rather affected a plainness of garb, and aversion to the magnificence which desecrates the humility of conscious magnanimity by the massive and ornamental display of architectural grandeur. Their designs are confined more to utilitarian purposes than the efforts of sublime and stupendous genius or the *beaux arts*. Each man is an Agesilaus in himself, and values his coarse rude national habit, the unsightly produce of a semibarbarous loom, far above those exquisite elaborations, the nice and sumptuous fabrics of superb refinement. When they have decorated their females with the voluptuous fascinations of " barbaric pearl and saint-seducing gold," and ornamented their horses with similar and appropriate adjuvants of emblazoning display, desire and covetousness are sufficiently inflamed and gratified by the survey of opulence. The pompous embellishments of art they prefer to hold in extraneous honour, whilst iron war and the vehement pursuits of savage heroes fill up the fiercer attributes of their ferocious enjoyments.

The Ameer was not attended by a guard of regular troops, but his personal servants, many of whom were confidential household slaves, came armed into his presence. Every day, except Thursday morning, he sat in public to transact business. Thursday morning was devoted to the bath until 10 o'clock; after this hour those only visited him who were called. He usually employed the time before noon in auditing his domestic affairs in company with his mirzas or writers. His senior brother, Nawaub Jubbar Khan, and the eldest among his nephews, who was a contemporary in age with himself, and highly respected by him for the profound practical wisdom of his measures, the Nawaub Mahomed Zeman Khan, were accustomed to pay their respects early in the morning on ordinary days. The first named was less formal, and generally went to durbar* every day. The other was a valetudinarian, and being fond of the etiquette of forms, would urge his ill health as an excuse for not appearing in public more frequently. The Ameer never adopted any important measure without consulting Nawaub Zeman Khan. This Nawaub has, since the expulsion of the English from Cabul, been made Shujah ul Moolk's vizier. He is a profound politician, but still of benevolent reputation, and the possession or affectation of many estimable virtues may be placed amongst the evidences of his wisdom. Friday was appropriated to the promiscuous access of the populace. On this day the gateway of his durbar was thrown wide open, and the doorkeepers withdrawn. Every one who had a cause to urge or curiosity to gratify might come into the presence without impediment. The Ameer heard all complaints in person, attended by the Cauzee. Civil causes were referred to this functionary for judgment, and the sentence was enforced by the Ameer. Criminal causes which were not likely to yield a fine, were also referred to the Cauzee, to shift from his own shoulders the odium of an onerous act. He never hesitated enforcing the Ooriff law, when he could do so without encroaching upon or curtailing the privileges of the oligarchy. The Ooriff is the law of usage administered by secular authority. But as the Sherrah, or written law of Mahomed, the rule for all Mahomedan communities, is the only legal polity, the Ooriff is an usurpation of might, founded in the absolute will of the prince in his secular character, and when the ability to enforce his edicts ceases to

---

* The levee.

exist, the Sherrah resumes its force, and may be effectually appealed to, superseding by its award the decrees of an usurped power. If the prince chooses to violate the Sherrah, he acts upon his individual responsibility; his judgments when oppressive are invasions of popular rights, and consequently a tyranny which is only yielded to by the obsequious necessity of present evil.

The remainder of the week was employed in the transaction of miscellaneous business. The hours of business were confined to the forenoon. His highness, in common with all Mahomedans, was an early riser, which custom is necessary to admit of the performance of the prescribed morning prayers. Of the five periods of prayer commanded by the traditionary law, the first must be finished before sunrise, otherwise the act becomes "guzzah," or "lapsed;" in this event the prayer is unacceptable to the Deity, or of no avail; and the consequences attending neglect of religious duty should be deprecated by charitable donation, at least to the provision of a meal for the necessitous. Conscientious persons will perform this penitential hospitality, though the mass of the community are indifferent to the pious injunction. After the conclusion of this first religious duty, which commences the diurnal service and routine of life, he read a few pages in the Koran attended by his Immaum. This functionary translated into Persian, or rather expounded in that colloquial dialect, the Arabic of the sacred volume, which the Mosleman hold to be the Word of God. In this employment he would be engaged an hour, more or less, as the task was longer or shorter. At the conclusion of this matin exercise, to which all the faithful, who have singular pretensions to piety, are addicted, the chiefs who composed the durbar made their entree promiscuously, and, with the simple ceremony of a bow, and the ordinary salutation " Usulam Allaikoom," touching the forehead as they leaned forward with the inner surface of the four fingers of the right hand, took their seats on the right or left of his highness. They were seated generally according to the rank of each guest. There was a master of ceremonies, called " Ishk Aughassee," (pronounced Shaugassee,) with a long official wand of olive wood, turned and lacquered yellow; upon this he leaned when unoccupied, at the entrance into the presence chamber, facing the Ameer in a standing attitude. When a Sirdar appeared he conducted him to his appropriate place, or in case some one of inferior dignity preoccupied the position, he caused the locality to be vacated for the accommodation of the pretender whose right was incontestable; and the claim of either was indicated by his rank or the favour in which he stood at court. The Ameer arose to receive his brother and the Nawaub Mahomed Zeman Khan. To others of high repute he would rise upon his knees, or make an effort to do so, which merely seemed like an inclination of the body.

The salutation of every one was returned by an audible response, it being amongst the religious injunctions of the faithful to reply to proferred civility a reciprocal acknowledgment. They are probably just in the estimation of politeness when they ascribe humility and condescension to the courteous. These are qualities which all profess to admire and endeavour to practise, notwithstanding the exclusive bigotry of pure Mahomedanism. My place in durbar was alongside of the Ameer, on the left, if the right should be preoccupied, otherwise on the right. If his brother, the Nawaub, was there when I entered, he always gave place to me. The Nawaubs Jubbar Khan and Mahomed Zeman Khan, and Sirdar Golam Mahomed Khan Populzye, whose daughter was married to the heir apparent, and myself, were the only officers who enjoyed the prescriptive right of seating ourselves on the same numed or felt which his highness occupied. When the heir apparent was present he did so also, but generally at the extremity of the high place at a little distance from his father: then I always strove to sit below him; but this was an action the young prince affably dispensed with, and usually commanded me to sit nearer the Ameer than himself. As the Ameer's aid-de-camp and general of his regular troops, I possessed the rank of a chief Sirdar; and his highness was ever pleased when I appeared in his suite, either in his afternoon rides, which he was accustomed to take for recreation, or in the morning durbar, when he sat for the transaction of business. About 11 o'clock, A. M., the people and officials, suitors and attendants, were dismissed, with the exception of those who usually ate in company with his highness, and breakfast was served in. These guests were, his brother, one or two of his chief counsellors, and myself, who familiarized ourselves with the Ameer by partaking of the same dish with his highness. The attachés of the durbar, of rank and dignity becoming the princely hospitality, one or two of his principal secretaries and feudal lords in confidential employment, assisted at the next dish of pillao placed on the cloth below the Ameer. Men of inferior dignity, though respectable, as persons of official rank, gathered around a third kab or plate of pillao, and a fourth and fifth detachment, the last of whom might be the fiddlers, huddled together over the lowest dish, which was cooked, in reference to its debased position, with very little ghee, (melted butter,) and probably without the viand. The standing dish is a pillao made of rice and meat, usually mutton, sometimes fowl. There were ragouts of fowl and partridges; soup, boiled potherbs, pickles, and preserves: a large bowl of sherbet occupied the middle of the feast. Our bread was leavened, and formed into a flat round cake, a foot in diameter, and an inch thick, grooved at intervals with ridges about two fingers broad and served as a plate; it was excellent, and highly creditable to the Cabul bakers, as the whole feast was to the *cuisine* of the "artiste" who manipulated the comestibles. The cooks are natives of Cashmere, and their system is Persian, with the embellishments of Cashmerian ingenuity in the invention, service, and concoction of delicious preparations, not surpassed by those superb Frenchmen who have thought themselves unrivalled in the science of *Potology*. The whole was despatched in half an hour, and the servants, whose portion was the remnants of the meal, not unfrequently confounded the moral of the old saw "the latter end of a feast is better than the beginning of a fray," as with them these extremes of hate and love, of hostility and hospitality, were identified in synonymous measure. The servants who removed the dishes devoured their broken contents with the voracity of kites and vultures on the wing. Scarcely out of the presence, the morsels of food were gobbled up with the appetite of struggling hunger in contending feud.

When recent spring fruit came into season the Ameer frequently breakfasted at nine o'clock, on mulberries or apricots, in which instance he usually abstained from the more solid repast at meridian. The peculiar attribute of the Cabul climate and alpine topography, is the contemporaneous prevalence of all the spring fruits at one period; the first ripened continuing in perfection throughout the season—the various modifications and different exposure of the valleys and glens affording a versatility of temperature that produces the effect of a progressive season, marked by the maturity of abundant and delicious fructification. At twelve o'clock, the Prince and the élite retired and slept until two P. M.; at this hour they arose to perform the second prayer. After his ablutions and toilet the Ameer egressed from his haram, and mounting his horse, which was in waiting at the gateway, he sallied out upon his evening ride. He had a fondness for fine horses, and generally visited his stud in the afternoon; but this occupation was more appropriate to the spring, when the brood mares and colts attracted his regard, and participated in his care. In the summer and fall he luxuriated in the picturesque scenery about the city from a favourite prospect point; seated himself, with a few select friends, on the bank of a running stream, of which there were several about the vicinity, and enjoyed a cup of tea; or visited some one of the magnificent, ornamental, and useful gardens near the suburbs of Cabul, accompanied by a train of musicians. In the spring he viewed his stud daily about three or four P. M. He sat on a terrace made for the purpose, two or three feet high, covered with felts. Here many of his chiefs joined him who did not usually attend in morning durbar. These were stipendiary lords, and moolahs or priests and familiar friends who enjoyed his confidence; they passed their time in smoking the cullioon,* desultory conversation, complimentary commendations of the prince's unique fancy for horses, and admiration of the promising brood of young colts, which were the delight of his highness and favourites of his taste. These companions passed the evening with his highness until he retired. He returned to his Derri Khaneh (place of durbar) at nightfall. Having previously performed the third prayer, he mounted his horse and moved into quarters. The evenings, when the weather permitted were passed in a beautiful flower garden: we sat on a low terrace illuminated by a large lamp. During the season of full bloom, the position was surrounded by an invisible and delightful fragrance of the ever wakeful floral nature; the intoxicating perfume of the rose, the spicy pink breathing of sweetness, and the flood of grateful odour that bathed the senses from the enchanting "shubboo."† The genial air of midsummer, tempered by the everlasting Alps of permanent snow near the valley, gratefully clothed our nocturnal hours in a voluptuous mantle of serene repose. The music was there too, fitful, frantic, or pathetic, as the feast of reason and the flow of soul invoked its mysterious influence which,

> "Softly sweet in *Persian* measure,
> Gently soothed the soul to pleasure."

Cabul, the city of a thousand gardens, in those days was a paradise far removed from the agitating

* Persian water pipe.
†"Or nocturnal odour;" the July or Jilly flower, that sheds its scent after nightfall, is so called by the Persians.

scenes of life away from the world. In the remotest mountain glens and vales of the "frosty Caucasus," devoted to the fairy conceptions of imaginative romance, there the soul of love sighed not but luxuriated in the delicious exuberance of ideality, and associated in fellowship with the nightingale, whose only dream was of carnation roses and Cupid gambolling in a bed of pansies, and who sang so sweetly in her vesper song of never dying happiness in love's uninvaded bower. And I have seen this country, sacred to the harmony of hallowed solitude, desecrated by the rude intrusion of senseless stranger boors, vile in habits, infamous in vulgar tastes—the prompt and apathetic instruments of master minds, callous leaders in the sanguinary march of heedless conquests, who crushed the feeble heart and hushed the merry voice of mirth, hilarity, and joy. To return to the Ameer. His highness kept very late hours, particularly during the long nights of winter. I have repeatedly sat up with him until three A. M. Dinner was brought after "usser," or the fourth prayer, which shortly followed sunset. This meal similar to the breakfast was served sooner or later, generally before eight o'clock, as his appetite suggested, although sometimes deferred until ten o'clock. When this was the case, fresh fruit would be introduced about eight, and the intermediate time was passed by his highness playing several games of chess with Cauzee Budder u'Deen, or in conversation. When his highness was engaged at chess the conversation ceased, and the interlocutors gathered nearer the performers, to observe the game, and applaud the sagacity he displayed. I never knew him lose a game. The Cauzee was always beaten. At the conclusion of each game the science of certain moves was discussed, and a sufficient amount of flattery bestowed on the unrivalled play of his highness. Notwithstanding, the wily Avghans would aside pass winks and gestures from one to another, and occasionally some one, more privileged than the rest, has been heard to taunt the Ameer, by hinting that the Cauzee played bad intentionally, and lost to flatter him. He took this rallying always in good part, and it is certain that the Cauzee was much too complaisant ever to gain a game even by chance.

These nocturnal parties were conducted with perfect regard to etiquette and good manners. He was fond of listening to the relation of travels, and allusions to history; made frequent inquiries of merchants who were known to visit distant countries, concerning the manners and customs of the people they had seen, the character of the prince, the government, religion, and particularly, geography and topography, for which sciences he seemed to have a strong inclination. He was well acquainted with the Russian military system, and the best account, detailed with accuracy and illustrative minuteness, I have heard of the destruction of the janissaries by the last Sooltaun of Turkey, was recited to me by the Ameer. He was much addicted to telling stories of his personal adventures; he delighted to talk of himself, was pleased with his own declamation, and vain of his eloquence. If merit is to elicit the award of praise, he was justly entitled to admiration for the ready command of language and agreeable mode of displaying his talents in colloquial intercourse. Buffoonery never formed a part of his princely amusements, but refinement of moral or purity of design did not always characterize the tenor of his *improvisatore*. His anecdotes were not unfrequently gross and sensual. Unsophisticated by the arts of intellectuality, he thought that " nature unadorned was adorned the most." No event lost by relating any importance in reality, or was obscured by the nomenclature of modesty. He dealt a good deal in sarcasm, and was ever ready to trump his adversary's trick. Ridicule was a weapon that he flourished with considerable effect, and he could good-humouredly make himself or his position the subject of ludicrous wit. The demands of his courtiers, or rather the feudal lords who represented the communities and constituted the most powerful element of the government, kept the Ameer always greatly straitened for the resources of present means, and I have heard him make his poverty, which really arose from extreme circumspection in providing for the necessities of personal defence out of his civil list, the source of ridicule. He alluded to the rapacity of the Avghans, and made himself the object of derision. " We are," said his highness, addressing himself to me, " like the hungry fox, of whom you may have heard?" I assured him I had not, and begged to be indulged with the relation.

" The Avghans know the story well," he continued: " there was a miserable, half-starved fox, who lived or rather famished in the mountains about Cabul, where you know the inhabitants seek their bread in the bowels of a rock. He had been unsuccessfully prowling about all night in search of food, and was reluctantly, and faint with the despondence of disappointed hope, obliged about daylight to slink away towards his hiding-place,—snarling, growling, and madly snapping at the oblique rays of the rising sun, that glanced in his worried eyes, displacing the shade of early day; he trotted on sullenly and forlorn with the pains and impatient violence of hunger. Reflecting on the misfortunes of his destiny, he suddenly came face to face with a large ram of the broad-tailed breed. No salutation greeted the interview; one was predetermined to see an enemy in every casual rencontre, and the other never cared, for he was accustomed to doubts and *buts*, to make acquaintance with strangers; and he grazed alone, and nibbled the soft grass, and licked the morning dew as he browsed in solitary independence. Reynard stopped and eyed him with a strong desire to seize hold of his throat; but natural timidity constrained him to avoid the attempt. Looking wistfully after him as he slowly moved away, the fox was astounded to see the large pendulous tail, which appeared like a load of flesh, dangling precariously, and on the point of falling from its attachment. New hopes kindled in his hungry stomach, and he stole softly after the ram, expecting the momentary descent of the excrescence which seemed so useless to the owner and desirable to himself. He thought the ram was ready enough to get rid of the tail, for he shook it more vigorously than usual that day. Reynard ever and anon started forward to seize the prize, which at every step gave promise, by its oscillating and frequent motion, and rapid and sudden gyrations, of an immediate meal. Now the ram stamped angrily, and evinced extreme impatience; his tail vibrated, and the fox, in breathless desire, and desperate with hunger, felt, or thought he felt, the morsel between his teeth. Still the tail hung on, and the expectant fox, with renewed allurements, kept on the track of the ram, who went slowly and quietly browsing along the whole day. At length reaching his fold he walked in, and left the disappointed fox, hungry and hopeless, standing at the door. So the day passed off, Reynard's wants becoming insupportably urgent; and this starving prototype of the famished Avghans suspended the cravings of his stomach by gnawing at an old cast-off shoe of the shepherds, or some such insufficient fare, and went away trusting to Providence. Now this is just my condition," added his highness, with a vociferous laugh; " I shall be looking after this European agent in momentary expectation of something falling from him, and eventually turn away like the miserable fox, to feed on the hard fare which has always been the lot of us mountaineers. As well might the fox have looked for the descent of the ram's tail, as I anticipate pecuniary assistance from this Feringee. But what of that? Thanks and praise be to God, the Creator of all things, we are not without an intercessor in the divine mercy."

In his dress the Ameer affects plainness. His apparel is that of a Dooraunee gentleman, of a liberal establishment, without any distinctive designation. He was much attached to horses, and always desired to have fine animals of the first breed. He had many splendid saddle horses from the most celebrated marts of Toorkistaun, and a few Arabs; he had also a fine charger from Khoordistaun, of a dappled iron gray colour, which I think was the prettiest of all his stud.

The Ameer never appears armed except on a journey. In the ordinary intercourse of society, the Dooraunee chiefs do not wear arms; but they are all accustomed to do so when travelling. The Nawaub

Jubbar Khan formed an exception to this general remark. I never saw him armed on a journey, though I have repeatedly accompanied him on excursions. When in the presence of a hostile army he came into the field as an ambassador, conjointly with myself, which was the only occasion on which I ever saw him armed, he wore, in a plain scabbard, a Persian sword, which is said to have cost ten thousand rupees.*

As Ameer ul Momineen or commander of the fathful, the example of sobriety, humility, and justice was incumbent on Dost Mahomed, all of which he attempted, and thereby gave occasion to inquisitive persons to stigmatize his character with the charge of hypocrisy, for he was vain, rapacious, and perfidious. His highness also professes to have great veneration for religion, and accordingly displays a show of respect for the ulima or professors of Mahomedan law. He has promulgated religious wars against the Seiks, and sworn eternal enmity to their race; he has coined money in his own name as an independent prince, the inscription pledging him to an exterminating system of war with his infidel neighbours, which principle would carry him much farther than Lahore; for after having conquered the Seiks, there is China next to employ the arms of the faithful, and also the British power in India. The capacity of his mind, or rather the bigotry of his superstition, presents a comprehensive and invincible response to every doubt. "All infidels are alike to the faithful, and before God there is nothing impossible." Nawaub Mahomed Zeman Khan, his chief privy counsellor, expressed his opinion that

* Five thousand dollars.

the sole object of the Ameer's intrigues with the Russians, Persians, and English, was to extract money from either or every one of those parties, which he would instantly have expended in a crusade against the Seiks, for the conquest of Peshour. He made a religious war the pretext to animate popular feeling, and directed the excitement through a surreptitious channel, towards the establishment of political views. That he was not so devoted to the principles of Islam as to keep only in mind the object of a religious war was evident from the fact of his proposing pacific terms to Runjeet'h, on condition of receiving Peshour; and this he did when I visited his camp as ambassador from the court of Lahore. His highness was then approaching that city with an army of fifty thousand musketeers, in the spring of 1835. This army consisted chiefly of the militia, comprising a large portion of the undisciplined but able-bodied populace of his principality. He boasted to me that he was followed by one hundred thousand armed men at the moment I entered his camp, and I remarked "If the Prince of Panjab (Runjeet'h) chose to assemble the militia of his dominions, he could bring ten times the number into the field; but you will have regular troops to fight, when you contend against Runjeet'h's forces, and your *sans culotte* militia will vanish like mist before the sun."

I spoke in an exalted strain of the efficiency of the Seik army, and displayed the wealth and military force of Runjeet'h in a light which made the Ameer's spirit recoil. He lost his temper, which he readily did, and became enraged, and then his eyes glared upon me as he replied with a characteristic shake of the head, and elevated brows, all of which was to indicate a reckless wilfulness of design: "Your appearance in the midst of my camp at this moment of general excitement may be attended with personal danger. When Secunder (Alexander) visited this country, he sent a confidential agent to the prince hereabout, and the mountaineers murdered Secunder's ambassador!" Feeling myself strong in the friendship of his brothers, and intimacy of his most influential chiefs, I answered roughly and without hesitating, "I am not accredited to you, but to your brother, who is now a guest amongst you as I am myself." This expression, which intimated my knowledge of the discord prevailing in his domestic affairs, exasperated the Ameer to say, "My brother!—who is the brother independent of my will? Is not the policy of my court controlled by myself, that the enemy sends an ambassador to another in the midst of my camp? Know that I am all in all!" and upon this arrogant pretension I planned and accomplished his defeat. I did not fail subsequently to draw the attention of his brother to the assertion of supremacy by the Ameer, and the detriment to his personal dignity and political importance compromised by that assumption. It was evident his highness no longer considered his brother a party in his negotiations with the Seiks, and that if Runjeet'h gave up to the Ameer the city of Peshour, his highness would retain the acquisition on his own account, and not, as he fancied, procure the cession for him.* His best

---

* This brother, who was Sooltaun Mahomed Khan, was then lately deprived of Peshour by Runjeet'h, and had thrown himself on the hospitality of Dost Mahomed to solicit his assistance in the endeavour to drive out the Seiks. The Ameer readily approached Peshour with that ostensible purpose, but secretly with the motive of gaining the city for himself by any possible means.

plan would be to anticipate the Ameer, who was in secret communication with Runjeet'h, and go over at once to the Prince of Lahore, who would receive him munificently, and satisfy him in all his hopes; for there was now evidence that the Ameer only coveted Peshour, without being actuated by religious feeling against the Seiks; and was treating clandestinely for the purpose. The knowledge of this fact also caused many of his followers to disperse. I encouraged the Ameer's expectation that Runjeet'h might be induced to relinquish Peshour, which kept him from throwing away his resources on the hungry retainers who followed his standard. Many of them in consequence withdrew, and as has already been related, his brother confirmed the defection—changing position on the board, and castling with the King of Lahore.

When the Ameer was engaged in military demonstrations he kept up more state than at other times. He had an extensive suite of tents, capable of accommodating his durbar. He gave audience seated at the upper end of a large double-poled tent, one side of which opened into an area included within extemporaneous walls of party-coloured canvass. These were set up to screen the occupants from public gaze. The hour of marching was designated by the Ameer, and the army moved off generally about daybreak. On the march he was accompanied by a body of irregular cavalry, constituted of the confidential retainers; his personal guard, his domestic establishment, composed of the pesh khidmuts,* household slaves, and most trustworthy military adherents, all of

* Body servants.

whom are styled "Umilah i Khwass," or select retainers. Many of the feudal lords, brothers, counsellors, and subordinate chiefs, with their immediate responsible servants, also swelled the cavalcade and added the imposing dignity of numbers to the promiscuous and undisciplined swarms of cavalry, each band being designated by a discriminating banner and preceded by kettle-drums at the saddle-bow of the "Duff Nowaz."*

> The shrill trumpet's blast and the drum's deep roll,
> The towering plume and the prancing steeds,
> Then clamour'd afar to the soldier's soul
> Gallantry, glory, and chivalrous deeds.

His highness held a levee for half an hour after reaching his tent, when the durbar was dismissed; and in the afternoon about three o'clock the principal chiefs, and every one who may have a feasible representation to prefer, present themselves and are admitted. The Ameer, although always accessible, was still more so when surrounded by his army in the field than in quarters. They retired within two hours, and assembled again after the prayer of "Usser," at sunset.

Smoking the cullioon was always an interlude of frequent recurring instance, and the fumes of the weed enveloped with ominous clouds the thoughtful conclave, when excitement swept over the nerves; deep inspirations of the bland sedative subduing the solicitude of care. The Persian pipe was replenished and passed round at brief intervals upon all abstruse occasions. Many an abstract idea seems to have

---

* The person who sounds the kettle-drum. He is usually the barber, *en cavalier.*

found a buoyant medium in " the smoke that so gracefully curled" from the human mouth divine, and as the lips propelled the vapour, the tongue vapoured in turn. Boasting, indeed, is one of the essential elements of Asiatic bravery, the most forcible proof the Ameer could instance of dubious fidelity on the part of a craven chief was " he never boasted of prospective success during the whole period of his service in camp."

The company that dines with the Ameer when in the field is not so *recherché* as usual, inasmuch as any one of respectable pretensions may make an effort to stay when an attendant announces the meal, which has been previously called for by the Ameer, and if the place was not crowded with his superiors, would passively be allowed by the servants to thrust his fist into the everlasting pillao. In case of a multitude, the small folk would be ordered out by the master of ceremonies, to give place for others of higher rank. Most of the khans or chiefs usually dine in their own tents. This is expected by their retainers, who have better fare from the remnants of their leader's hospitality than their ordinary allowance. Those who retire, or remain at home to dine, call on the Ameer subsequently. The food of his highness is prepared by responsible servants, and he carefully abstains from partaking of a collation provided by any one else; neither will his brothers participate in a preparation procured from his establishment, unless it has been provided for the Ameer, and first tasted by his highness. In company with Sooltaun Mahomed Khan, I arrived in the Khyber defile at the Ameer's tent one day later than ordinary, after the durbar had been dismissed, and the breakfast despatched. Civility required that food should be placed before the Ameer's brother. All comestibles of the *cuisine* had been removed; but preserves, and bread, and cheese were proffered, which Sooltaun Mahomed declined with acknowledgments of the hospitality. His attendants did the practical honours to the feast; but the day being exceedingly hot, and the Sirdar extremely thirsty from fatigue and exposure to the sun, was invited by the Ameer to take a drink of *Doug*.* The brother hesitatingly declined the proposed kindness; but the Ameer importuned him, and forthwith ordered a servant who was in waiting to produce the beverage. It was brought instantly, and as the subordinate approached with it, Sooltaun Mahomed motioned him to hand the bowl, containing the doug, to the Ameer. The Ameer excused himself, saying, " I have breakfasted, lalla ;† help yourself." Then commenced a scene of protestation and importunity which lasted several moments; at length Sooltaun Mahomed observed, " Impossible, brother; it's not possible for me to take it until you have first refreshed yourself," and so, notwithstanding his highness was not at all thirsty, his brother, by the pretext of hospitality, assured himself of the salutary condition of the proffered bowl, by first obliging the host to drink, which he did freely, and then transferred it to his guest. I drank from the same bowl and of the identical contents with which the princes refreshed themselves, and add my testimony to what I have frequently heard expressed, that sour milk

---

* This is sour milk not skimmed. It is fresh milk prepared by a premature process of souring, and then made into a homogeneous fluid by thorough shaking in a leather bag.

† Brother.

surpasses any other beverage to quench thirst in a sultry climate on a hot day.

The Ameer is styled by his flatterers commander of the faithful; but that title belongs only to the Sooltaun of Turkey, called by the Mahomedans Sooltaun of Room. The sooltaun is the head of the Mosleman religion; he derives his sacred character from his ancestor, the great Toghrul Beg, who was invested with the dignity of vicegerent of Mahomed, and commander of the faithful, by the Khalif of Baghdad, (according to D'Herbelot,) in the year 1057, A. D., or 448 of the Mahomedan year, in the month Zul Kaadeh, and twenty-fifth day thereof.

The Ameer professes great regard for religion; he strictly conforms to the prescribed rules of prayer, observes the fasts, the ceremonies, and rites which belong to the Mahomedan faith; but his practice, though generally conformable to oriental ideas of morality, is at variance with piety and equity. He believes in the orthodox principles of the Mahomedan religion, which are professed by the sect of Soonee, although his education in very early life must have given his mind a bias towards the sect of Sheah, of which schismatic persuasion his mother was a disciple.

Apparently he is not a bigoted Soonee, which circumstance rather favours the suspicion of his being inclined to the opposite creed. One of the principles of the Sheah sect is to inculcate and assert a false profession of their real tenets when in presence of the opposite schism; but the Soonee being an ardent and unyielding enthusiast, is called upon by his faith to assert his belief under every circumstance, and maintain his creed by the sword —the readiest, most potent, and effective argument that could be devised. All who deny the Prophet are infidels, deserving death, and their polemics prohibit discussions upon an article of faith. To argue is to imply a momentary concession of doubt, and this would be evidence of blasphemy, which calls for the instant expiation of blood. The Ameer is a fanatic in profession, but not a bigot in practice, which character confirms the charge of hypocrisy. He avoids the discussion of doctrinal points or religious matters no less amongst his own Moolahs* than Christians who may visit his court, and is noted for tact in turning a discourse which has a tendency to create irascible feelings on sacred subjects, even when he may not have been an interlocutor. He is remarkable for delicacy of expression, and politeness of modesty in argument on all subjects, and patient of contradiction even when delivered with asperity. He has no honesty in any sense, no morals, no piety; a liar in the completest sense of the word; subtle, cunning, timorous, and governed in all things, sacred and profane, political and civil, moral and physical, by interest, social, sensual, and avaricious interest: this word is the key to his character, the test of his motives. In pursuit of his interests he is crafty and unprincipled. His personal comfort he essays with recklessness of human suffering. His sensuality is unbounded, but offensive only to himself. Avarice is the motive that engrosses his soul. For the gratification of this abominable vice he cares not for the shedding of human blood; otherwise he is not cruel, although the greatest and most inhuman violence has been committed under his countenance and

* The clergy are so designated.

authority in the extortion of gold. Mercy is the least of all considerations with him, and he has never been known to act with clemency or generosity when the accumulation of gold was the question at issue. For the purpose of discovering suppositious or hidden wealth, torture was inflicted in barbarous and horrible forms, not unfrequently terminating in the death of the sufferer.

As a financier the Ameer's ideas were purely oriental. Our own politicians have said that the Toorks surpass in this respect their Christian neighbours, and are better fiscal agents than the systematic Europeans. Instances in illustration have been adduced, and the facility noticed with which the Grand Porte was able to pay an immense sum of tribute to Russia at a time when the resources of the empire were supposed to be totally exhausted. The space of time within which the operation was accomplished, astonished the politicians of Europe; nevertheless there is a great doubt whether their *method* of finance can be called *better* than our own : their fiscal economy is based on an agrarian system, and the increase of taxation falls suddenly and universally on an impoverished community, aggravating the national distress through individual misery out of all proportion to the amount of revenue derived. When the resources of the land revenue fail,—and they are frequently impaired by an unfavourable season or unexpected demand above the ordinary tribute,— the oriental princes, who are all despotic, mulct their subjects, and the scourge and bastinado are the instruments of fiscal economy, who lend their aid to extort the last pittance from the wretched cultivator of the soil. Thousands of the populace are reduced to poverty and extreme want, and many even sold into slavery to liquidate the demands of an exacting prince; and this has been the system of the East from the days of Pharaoh,—" when money failed in the land they brought their cattle," and when their herds and their flocks were also gone, they sold themselves into bondage. This has been the Turkish system for ages, and there is matter of amazement in reflecting on the resources of the Greeks, the wreck of whose dominions could for nearly four hundred years sustain the rapacity of these conquerors of the eastern empire, and the exhausting, destructive, depopulating, and unrenovating practices of the Toorks. This is the system which is now, and has been, from the beginning of their power in Europe, destroying that empire " without hand," as Daniel says. Upon the establishment of their power in Europe they became an agricultural and deteriorating community. They relinquished their principles of accumulation when they no longer remained a military and predatory people. The habits upon which their social system was based being those of rapine, war, and plunder, have remained in practice, whilst those self-destroying elements have had no other field for operation than their own possessions, and *felo de se* is their destiny, notwithstanding the conflict of England against fate in her policy of maintaining the integrity of the Ottoman empire; of sustaining the commander of the faithful, the vicegerent of Mahomed, " the man of fierce countenance, *who* magnified himself unto the prince of the host, *and* stood up against the prince of princes, he shall be broken without hand."

In regard to commerce, the Ameer was impressed with the advantages which encouragement of that sort of enterprise imparts to a country; but his necessities were of a nature to constrain his desire of acting with good faith towards the commercial community. The nominal duties were apportioned according to the injunctions of their great lawgiver; the tariff was two and a half per cent on the property of the faithful, and five upon that of infidels, levied ad valorem or specific at the option of the merchant, and in either instance received in kind. The claims of equity asserted by the trader were frequently overruled by the clamour of exigency, and pretexts were readily suggested to excuse extraordinary demands on the part of the prince. Open violence was avoided, and no justification allowed to the merchant for the charge of robbery, with which matter-of-fact persons, who contemplated results more than the ostentatious display of assumed principles, were disposed to stigmatize the discrepancies of a necessitous financier. The Ameer would gain his object through the medium of friendship and brotherhood, consistently with the Persian policy, " if you would ruin any one, first become his friend,"—*par example:* his highness never hesitated inviting himself to an evening visit at the house of a wealthy merchant, when with profuse protestations of regard, amongst which the words " friend" and " brother" were prominent, he modestly begged a loan on a quantity of household jewels. The merchant, who comprehended the whole process of finesse which his highness had in reserve, immediately proposed to lend the money on the Ameer's note of hand or his honour; preferring to make a merit of necessity, he wished to seem gratuitously complying and liberal, when he knew that if he accepted the jewels as security from the prince, the ruling power in the haram would bully them out of his possession; for as the wife would solicit the jewels, to whom could the merchant appeal? To the prince! Complain to the prince of his own favourite wife! Etiquette forbade the proceeding, and *might* recommended submissive despair. Hours have sometimes passed in these visits, lengthened out by the prince calling for tea, and smoking the callioon; and there he sat, with the comfortable familiarity of a welcome guest, provokingly condescending in pertinacious design, the host feeling like the bird with a blacksnake in its nest, vainly struggling with the fatal fascination of his intrusive guest. When every imaginable subterfuge had been fruitlessly attempted by the victim of avarice, exhausted with his own exertions he was drawn in like a trout on a line in the hands of an expert and patient sportsman; he saw with fish-eyed apathy his golden scales depart, and blessed his happiness in the salvation of his skin; for the Ameer neither killed nor skinned when the fish relinquished his scales, but slipped the *fin'd* animal into his element again, where he repaired at leisure the rubs of destiny.

Such is the Ameer Dost Mahomed, whom the English lately deposed from the sovereignty of Cabul. There is no doubt that in doing so they widely deviated from the line of prudence, and involved themselves in a policy which has already cost millions to establish, and will cost many millions to sustain. The Avghans, who are deeply interested in the late political events, which have given a new character to the Indo-British empire, have been driven by a system of perfidy, oppression, and false faith to the extremity of social misery. An independent community, which under the oligarchical form of Dost Mahomed's government, possessed the freedom to which they have always been accustomed, was subjected to an unlimited military despotism, and kept in subjugation by the British bayonet; their stronghold garrisoned by a foreign army; their religious and political institutions subverted, and their country conquered by an infidel power. But the possession of Avghanistaun by England has been transient and probationary of the oppressed.

Note.—That the English agent left Cabul without having arranged a treaty with Dost Mahomed, which should have secured the friendship of the Avghans, was certainly not owing to any aversion on the part of the Ameer. When the didactic and imperative ultimatum of Lord Auckland was handed to the Ameer, in which his highness saw the frustration of his hopes, for he was decidedly in favour of an English alliance, although he allowed his policy to be swayed by the Kizzlebashe or Persian interest, a general council was called. The document was handed to me amongst others; I satisfied myself, by the Governor-General's signature, of its authenticity, surveying the contents with extreme surprise and disappointment. Dost Mahomed was mortified, but not terrified. He always reassured himself that he had no occasion for apprehending alarm from the English, so long as Runjeet'h could maintain his independence. For to the native mind, the possession of power, without the exertion of authority is tantamount to imbecility, and the mere existence of the Panjab as an independent principality in the presence of a powerful neighbour, was indubitable evidence of that neighbour's unsustained repute. His highness never conceived that the English, who have great celebrity for utilitarian operations in their political enterprises, would project the invasion of Cabul through Kandhar, first subduing Scind, and surmounting the sterile wastes, the intricate mountain passes, and waterless deserts of Beloochistaun. The suffering to the troops and destruction of camp followers, and loss of baggage, recalls to mind the similar march of Alexander through Gedrosia, a part of the same country. A column of Alexander's army, returning from India, pursued this identical route, lately traversed by the army of the Indus. With the enemy at the gates of Cabul, the defection of his feudal chiefs, dissensions of his council, and desertions of his troops, all the result of British gold, and diplomatic promises, the obligarchy was dissolved, the ancient regime established and sustained by British bayonets, *absolutely without a contested campaign.*

The Governor-General's ultimatum was handed around, and an embarrassing silence ensued. A few minutes elapsed when Mirza Semme Khan recalled the party from abstraction. This individual, the leader of the Kizzlebashe party, had all along been remarkable for his asperity in combating the Prince's inclination towards the English alliance. He was of Persian descent and a schismatic Sheah, whose vindictive soul ever moved with enthusiastic hatred of the English, now opposed their agent, who had not bribed him to the full amount of his expectation. He proclaimed that the Governor-General's ultimatum left no other alternative than the dismission of the English agent, for the spirit of the Kizzlebashe party was supercilious and unyielding, though full of duplicity. The British negotiator made great promises to this influential body, no one of which was subsequently realized, and they were to a man not only exasperated to revenge the insult thus levelled at their community, which was of prætorian importance, but stimulated by the necessity of sustaining their order, and of providing for their subsistence, which had been cut off by the new form of government. Nieb Mahomed Ameer Khan Akhoond Zadah, who was an Avghan of the Barikzye tribe, stood high in the Ameer's estimation, and exercised great influence as the organ of the Avghan interest. He also held the appointment of Governor of Cabul, and was numbered amongst the chief supporters of the Ameer's family. He combined the character of a secretary of state, and a military chief. On this occasion he openly opposed the Kizzlebashe party, and urged many weighty arguments in favour of a pacific settlement of the Ameer's relations with the British government, which had now assumed a position so inauspicious, he concluded his oration with these words, addressing the Ameer, " Imkaun n'daried ta Shuma Harlan Sahebra der mean i een Sakhun N'aree bayed Kaeera, Nuzd i Burnes Saheb, b'freese, wo mokudimat i toora, az ukklewo, rah i Khood i ahel fering drust Kirda Khwahedad"—There is no other resource for you but to introduce Mr. Harlan in the negotiations with Mr. Burnes, and he, through his own facilities and wisdom, will arrange a treaty, according to their European usage, for the pacific and advantageous settlement of your affairs—and to this proposition the council *unanimously* assented. An official note was immediately despatched to Burnes's secretary, conveying intimation of the resolution, and by return of the messenger, an official response was received *indirectly declining* the proposition, by deferring the measure to a more convenient opportunity of time. The council dispersed, and I wrote to the English agent a letter, referring to the Ameer's previous official communication, investing me with power to treat, containing a proposal *to negotiate upon his own terms.* The reply I received was personally friendly, but I was much astounded that it evinced a deficiency of knowledge of first principles concerning the rights of independent powers in political negotiations. I could not have believed that a gentleman of liberal education, and ordinary talent for observation, was so totally ignorant of equity and the laws of nations as to make the assertions and pretext he urged to excuse and justify his refusal to recommence negotiations with the Ameer, although officially proposed upon his own terms! * * * * *

APPENDIX.

I.

The following extracts from The Atlas, an English paper of authentic resources, were written before the massacre of the Anglo-Indian army *en route* from Cabul to Jillalabad, but are still applicable to the state of affairs up to our last accounts in regard to Sale's position.

"With regard to our position at Jillalabad, reports of disasters and despair have been as abundant as they are at variance with each other. Our own correspondents seem to consider the gallant band under the command of General Sale at that place far from exposed to the imminent peril apprehended by some. There was no scarcity of provisions; there was a good supply of ammunition, and relief would, no doubt, be speedily afforded. The tone of the private letter on the subject published in last Saturday's Atlas, combined with the general tenor of others which have appeared in the columns of our contemporaries, will eminently tend, we trust, to allay the fears which we are led sanguinely to hope have been prematurely excited.

"Jillalabad is situated in lat. 34° 4' N., long. 70° 37' E., and lies about ninety miles due east of Cabul— the scene of the insurrection. The strength of our position was manifest, and tended to confirm the hope cherished of the perfect safety of our force in the fort, and their stout resistance in the event of a siege. A reperusal of the private letter published in our last would aid in still more clearly demonstrating the stirring scene."

"We have received several letters from our correspondents in India regarding the state of affairs in Avghanistaun. The following is an extract from one of them, which furnishes a graphic description of a stirring event:

" 'You will have heard of the clouded aspect of affairs in Avghanistaun—Sir Alexander Burnes murdered, with his brother and some other British officers; Sir W. M'Naghten, with half our troops, shut up in Cabul; General Sale, with the other half, shut up in Jillalabad; the whole country in arms; the passes closed, so that we only get occasional reports, with now and then a letter. The country had just been reported perfectly quiet by Sir A. Burnes. Sir W. M'Naghten, taking advantage, it is said, of such tranquillity, persuaded the imbecile shah to withhold the indulgence of a remission of revenue which the hill tribes had enjoyed time immemorial, as black mail, for keeping open the passes. These wild tribes flew to arms, and shut up, first the Khoord Cabul pass, which leads from Cabul to Jillalabad. Sale was sent to force it, which he did with great loss of officers and men. The Europeans were almost beaten. The enemy's loss was nothing; they closed on the rearguard and baggage; our sepoys behaved nobly. As soon as Sale cleared the pass it was closed in his rear, and he was cut off from Cabul with little ammunition or provision. The return was impossible in the face of the enemy, now grown bold by what must have been to them a victory. He fell back on Jillalabad, and, after giving up the cantonment, shut himself up with his little band in the walled town, where he was beleaguered. He appears to have made a successful sally until the 14th of November, particulars not known; but I learn that a body of 6,000 men were dispersed on the occasion. On the 1st instant (December) Azeez Khan invested the place with 4,000 men, who moved on to a general attack, confining themselves chiefly to the low broken grounds under the river bank. Their skirmishers crossed to within twenty yards of the walls, and even fired through our loopholes. They taunted us and defied us, (says my correspondent, who is one of the confined at Jillalabad), to come out, little thinking their request would so soon be complied with. At noon of the 15th the Cabul gate was thrown open, and out dashed 800 infantry, followed by 200 cavalry and two guns. The enemy broke ground and fled. The cavalry cut to pieces about 100 on the plain to the left. On the right, the infantry could not catch the fugitives, but, the ground being good, Captain Abbott took his guns forward at a gallop, and crossed their columns with a fire that sent them all down into the river's bed. Had the infantry now been able to close, the whole, or nearly the whole, of Azeez Khan's force, must have been cut to pieces. Captain Abbott now took his guns to the brink of the high bank which falls into the river, and made some excellent practice among the dense masses that crowded the fords. Many were killed, and more drowned by missing the fords in their haste. Sale now sent a peremptory order for retirement, and the troops fell back upon Jillalabad. The enemy showed symptoms of rallying, and a body of horsemen hovered at a distance upon our rear. The guns moved back to within 1400 yards, at which distance a round shot emptied two saddles, and compelled the whole gang to fly. A few more shot dispersed one or two other bodies, and our little band returned to Jillalabad. Shah Newaz Khan and another chief were killed in the cannonade, and about 300 small fry. The whole force decamped, and our friends expected eight or ten days' peace. Provisions were pouring in, and my correspondent speaks with great confidence of their safety, if means are taken in India for their timely relief. I give you a sketch of the scene, taken on the spot. It is roughly done, but explains affairs very clearly, notwithstanding the passes are not open. I know not how my correspondent's letter came. He says—' An attempt being made to send letters, &c. &c., I shall keep my journal for a safer opportunity.'

"' P.S. (21st Dec.)—Dost Mahomed has been caught intriguing with the rebels of Avghanistaun, telling them to hold out, for that he has passed through all the chief stations, and seen the troops. Thus the country is so drained for Avghanistaun that we cannot succour our countrymen; so that the rebels have only to put those down who are in the country, and the day is their own.' "

"The following is a copy of a letter from a private correspondent relative to our reverses in Avghanistaun. We give publicity to his remarks for two reasons—viz., on account of his former residence among the people of whom he speaks, and consequent knowledge of their character; and because the subject occupies much public attention at the present crisis:

"'The news from India by the last mail is certainly very appalling with respect to affairs in Avghanistaun, but just the style of thing I anticipated, and I do not see how it is possible to remedy the evil without immediate increase to the army.

"'My letters from Quettah mention that all is at present quiet there, and that a reinforcement of a wing of a Bombay regiment had arrived with some artillery. I very much fear, however, that the Avghan tribes in that neighbourhood will not remain passive, but join their brethren in rebellion, and render the passage of the Bolan more formidable than ever, and thus prove the policy of keeping an efficient brigade at Quettah. In that position the troops would be at once available for service towards Kandahar, but in their progress from Scinde, if opposed in the Bolan pass, would be sadly crippled before they reached Kandahar. A depôt of stores of every description should, in my opinion, be formed at Quettah in case of future need.

"'The tribe of Avghans called the Doomur Kakurs, attached to the Bolan rangers, have, I understand, absconded. This looks bad, and leaves a painful impression on my mind that the religious hatred of the Mahomedans towards the "Infidel Feringees" is more general than the many imagine.'"

II.

Illustration of a text from Daniel, xi. 45, showing the accordance of prophecy with history in reference to the Ottoman empire.

The following lecture on the present condition of Islam or the Mahomedan faith in Mosleman communities, has been traced out for the purpose of gratifying the laudable wishes of pious inquirers who have desired to be made acquainted with the points of Mahomedanism, corresponding with our Christian faith, in reference to the vital truths of prophecy that foretell the advent of Christ. The text I have selected suggests the importance of the inquiry, and leads us to consider this imposing subject in a view highly interesting to all men. The eleventh chapter of Daniel concludes with this sentence, " Yet he shall come to his end, and none shall help him;" and to elucidate this text, I propose offering a few remarks:

" Yet he shall come to his end, and none shall help him."—Daniel, xi. 45.

The affairs of the East, during several years, have occupied a prominent position in the field of European diplomacy. It is well known how much the attention of politicians has been engaged by events lately passed and still in progress in the Turkish empire, in Constantinople, Egypt, and Syria. The growing power, and the hostile attitude of Mahomed Ali Pasha, in relation to the head of the Ottoman empire, caused the Grand Porte to solicit the protection of Russia against the invasion of Egypt. The Emperor of Russia was enabled to afford with readiness and facility a guarantee against the threatened dangers of civil war, as the rebellion of Egypt would have been. The proximity of the Russian army, and the stipulations of treaties, offensive and defensive, existing between these powers presented the pretext for foreign interference. Constantinople was about to be placed under the control of Russian troops, and Russian policy would ultimately have reigned in the capital of the East. The city of Constantinople would have again become the seat of the Greek hierarchy; the Patriarch of the Greek church once more restored to the possession of his sacred rights and sacerdotal immunities; the cross, long prostrate beneath the crescent, exalted in its place; the venerated church of St. Sophia, whose dome was called the second heaven, and adored by the eastern Christians, purified from infidel pollution, would have been hailed by a grateful multitude of Christian pilgrims, and a flood of incidents followed, all bearing on the present dignity of the Christian church and the future welfare of Christianity. But the conflicting interests of England and Russia instigated the British government to assume an active part in the affairs of the East, and *the integrity of the Turkish empire*, the old ally of England, became a principle of their policy, which, to neutralize Russian influence at the Porte, the English pledged *themselves* with the courteous assistance of Austria and Prussia, to maintain. It is this principle, "the integrity of the Turkish empire," which constitutes the Eastern Question. The three other great European powers, France, Austria, and Prussia, were invited by

Russia and England to become parties to a treaty having for its object the integrity of the Turkish empire. But the doom of the Turks, so long the second wo of Christendom, was already written in prophetic characters, and the power of man abides not before the will of God.*

England's insufficient justification of her unchristian policy in using her arms for the resubjugation of Syria, a great part of whose population is of the Christian church, to a Mahomedan power, repelling Egypt and re-establishing the government of the Turks, the head of all Mahomedan communities, is a libel on the Christian name. It deserves our reprobation and calls for the vengeance of heaven. Why should not the Christian population of Syria also be permitted, like the Greeks, the privilege of forming an independent kingdom. The mountain districts of Syria are now in rebellion against the newly re-established power of their Mahomedan

---

* This Eastern Question is, probably, one amongst many other palpable causes (of which the cholera was also one) arising from the relations of Europe with the East that operates to suspend the judgments of the four angels represented in the vision of John: "I saw four angels standing on the four corners of the earth, holding the four winds of the earth, that the wind should not blow on the earth, nor on the sea, nor on any tree. *And I saw another angel ascending from the East*, having the seal of the living God, and he cried with a loud voice to the four angels to whom it was given to hurt the earth and the sea, saying, Hurt not the earth, neither the sea, nor the trees, till we have sealed the servants of our God in their foreheads. And I heard the number of them who were sealed: and there were sealed an hundred and forty-four thousand of *all the tribes of the children of Israel*."—Rev. vii. 1—4. These causes will continue in force until the reorganization of the Jewish nation, and the restoration of the twelve tribes must precede the general war predicted as the immediate consequence of *the time of the end* of Mahomedanism, or destruction of Islam, by the cessation of Turkish rule.

rulers, and the Sooltaun has never been equal to the conquest of these refractory mountaineers. Has justice ceased upon the earth, and shall Syria be again enslaved by the Turkish wo? Syria, upon whose shores *our* common ancestors toiled and fought for the honour of the church, and sweat blood upon the sterile sands of an imploring nation, with the motto upon their banners "Vult Deus," it is the will of God—Syria, so dear to the reminiscences of every Christian; a name now despised, dishonoured, polluted, and desecrated by infidel rule, oppressed by the Moslem race, who are abetted and sustained in their tyrannies by the descendants of Cœur de Lion, that warrior of the faith who contemned a kingdom for the conquest of a Saviour's tomb—by England, whose holy wars in Palestine attested the noble enthusiasm of a Christian host, who, led by the master-spirit of chivalry, failed not, in the inhospitable and desert wilderness, to rally at the beseeching voice of Christian crying unto Christian. But the days of Cœur de Lion are passed away; the chivalry of Malta is extinct, though England still retains the title of "Defender of the faith," which, with her Oriental policy, seems a mockery of *our* forefathers. Defender of the faith indeed she is; truly may England's Queen be termed commander of the faithful, from her protecting influence upon the integrity of the Turkish empire. We lament that the days are past when Europe once emptied her population into Asia in crusades against the *false* prophet. The flame of enthusiasm is superseded by the pen of diplomacy; the battles of the faith, no longer urged by ardent votaries, are left to the management of cool deliberate expediency; and the interests of Christianity are compromised by the commercial relations of modern states. Anticipated terror of Russian supremacy drives the British government into a system of dishonourable policy that confounds the church with secular interests, wickedly preferring these to the awful responsibility entailed by the command of Christ, and the hereditary behests of our ancestors.* The five great powers of the evangelized world strive for the maintenance of the Moslem pestilence, and their object is, *the integrity of the Turkish empire;* to assist and HELP the Sooltaun. " Yet he shall come to his end, and *none* shall help him." A short review of the present condition of Mahomedan governments, the causes of the decay of their political power, their traditions concerning the advent of the Saviour and the proximate dissolution of the Turkish empire, forcibly illustrates our text and several other passages of prophecy.

Before the final destruction of Mahomedanism it is said, Daniel, xi. 44, " But tidings out of the East and out of the *North*† shall trouble him."

---

* The fierce crusader's brandished spear,
The vengeful sword, the voice of seer
　We see, we hear, we feel no more.
Unhallowed age, unchasten'd race,
Would'st thou, dar'st thou, seek for grace,
　Behold the prophet's mystic lore.

† A line drawn from Constantinople to Pekin will divide the East betwixt England and Russia; the countries, excepting Persia, and it may now be added, Avghanistaun, south of the limit, falling to the former, whilst Russia emphatically rules in the north, without exception; her predominance in Persia exhibiting her political supremacy in the East no less than her geographical superiority. Of her prophetic position let the context speak.

From the repeated assaults which have been made by Russia on the north, by Persia and the rebellion of dependent provinces and vice-royalties on the east, the Turkish empire has become circumscribed almost within the walls of Constantinople, and her foreign relations now show this prophecy of Daniel has been fulfilled. We have seen also the Turks "go forth with great fury to destroy and utterly to make away many;" and how they have planted "the tabernacles of their palaces between the seas in the glorious holy mountain," in the late war of the Ottomans and their European allies against Egypt, Syria, Bagdad, and Damascus, which countries lie between the Mediterranean, the Black Sea, the Persian Gulf, and Red Sea; and we may calmly rest in the anticipation that the last sentence will be speedily followed out; "Yet he shall come to his *end*, and none shall help him." The period of the dissolution of the Turkish empire being nigh at hand—as we are taught by prophecy to believe, and by the history of the world to perceive and understand—it becomes an affair of the deepest interest to ascertain by the signs of the times the period *when* this important event is to take place, because the knowledge thereof forebodes a position of the world which involves the eternal happiness of mankind. The time of the event, however, it is not so important to be acquainted with, as the conviction of its certainty; because it is said, "Behold, I come as a thief;" consequently the exact time must be doubtful; we should therefore always be prepared. We are reproved by the Saviour for not observing coming events when indicated by the signs of the times; and if the political signs of these times lead us to a just inference of the probable speedy destruction of the Turkish empire, we shall be subject to the reproof of lukewarmness by allowing them to pass unnoticed; to the charge of apathy in reference to a condition of life which affects the salvation of our souls. Moreover, could we prove the period *now is* when he shall come to his end; by that result we should illuminate the dormant sense of prophecy, and illustrate the object for which the word of inspiration was given to the world; for it is written "the words are closed up and sealed till the time of the end;" Daniel, xii. 9; also verse 10th, " and none of the *wicked* shall understand, but the *wise* shall understand." How essential then that we should labour to understand, when the signs of the times solicit our attention, that we may not be numbered amongst those who shall not understand, but try to assume a position amongst the wise, who *shall* understand at the time of the end. I shall endeavour to show that by the present state of Islam, we are justified in the opinion of the time of the end being at hand; and the consequent awful responsibility we incur from indifference, and the moral obligation of inquiring into, and understanding as the wise shall understand.

It is one of the cardinal points of the Mahomedan faith that church and state cannot exist separately, and independent of each other. The principle is known in their commentaries and traditions by the epithet " Deen and Dunia," the first signifying religion and the ceremonies thereof, and Dunia their secular obligations. Their religion is intimately and systematically mixed up with their secular policy. The Sooltaun is the head of their religion, as he is of their government, and the authority of their chief, who is both Pope and Emperor, has been delegated with ceremonies of authentic investiture from Mahomed, the founder of their false doctrine; consequently, on the dissolution of the Ottoman empire, or cessation of *Turkish rule*, there will virtually and *prophetically* be a termination of the Moslem faith; and this religion must cease, with the political power, to exist as an independent principle in the social condition of the world.

It has been generally supposed that the reigning family of Constantinople is descended from the Prophet of Arabia. This belief is an error. The sooltaun is of Toorkey, not of Arab blood, as he should be if the reverse was true. He is the lineal representative of Toghrul Beg, a character well known in Oriental history, and famous in the annals of our ecclesiastical economy. Toghrul was a Tatar prince, who received the investiture of "commander of the faithful" from Ul Keim, the last of the Khuleefas, who reigned at Bagdad. On the ceremony of presentation, this prince, being advanced to the station of Mahomed's vicegerent upon earth, was decorated by Ul Keim with two swords —the sword of the faith and the sword of state. He received seven dresses of honour, and seven female slaves were conferred upon him, representing the "huft ukleem," or seven climates, a term which, in Asiatic phraseology, or imaginative geography, signifies the known world, over which the commander of the faithful was commissioned to hold dominion; and he was expressly charged with, and stimulated to, the conquest of the Christian powers of Europe. The descendants of Toghrul were subsequently, in prophetic language, bound in the Euphrates; and the princes of this dynasty represent, with their hosts, the four angels who were "prepared, for an hour and a day and a month and a year, for to slay the third part of man."

From the period of the last of the Khuleefas their power became hereditary in the family of Toghrul, and has been handed down through an uninterrupted and unprecedented succession of human glory to the present imbecile occupant of a tottering throne: this power may be deputed but cannot be usurped. Previous to the European conquests of the Turks, the flame of bigotry and Moslem enthusiasm raged with irresistible fury and overwhelming desolation. Empires were overthrown; dominions crushed; and the sword and Koran made the rule of social order throughout a great part of Asia, and several European kingdoms were also subjugated to Mahomedan sway; but from the period of the conquest of Constantinople by Mahmood ul Saney, (i. e. Mahmood the Second,) the high-strained principle of general intolerance that sustained and extended their faith has gradually declined, and the late innovations in jurisprudence and the military system of the Turks prove the official indifference of the commander of the faithful to the alleged sanctity of his national institutions. With the Turks to reform is to destroy, because the Koran, which is the base of all their laws, leaves no optional or discretionary power in the executive; neither is there any admission of a renovating process to repair the decay and oblivion of institutions stationary in the progressive march of mind;* the

---

* Thus Spain and other Roman Catholic countries, owing to their assumption of infallibility in religion, are still stationary in civilization, compared with the march of intellect evinced by the other kingdoms of Europe. Even France is oppressed with the Roman Catholic doctrine, which prevents the advance of civilization among nations no less than Mahomedanism.

prescriptions of the Koran are absolute, and should be administered now as they were ages past, when the star of the Prophet intensely glared upon the false professors of an apostate church, of a transgressing and idolatrous race. A public firman of the commander of the faithful has virtually displaced the authority of the Koran, and all religions are now, by the command of the Mahomedan Khuleefa or high priest, equal before the laws.

The population of the Moslem world is rapidly decreasing. The causes which produce this decay are evident to those acquainted with the laws, the manners, and the customs of the people. The tyrannical and oppressive system of fiscal policy, which deprives the peasant of all extraneous wealth, accruing from the utmost stretch of labour, and leaves merely the miserable portion of necessary rations for animal subsistence, is widely destructive of human life. The effect of polygamy in depopulating a community is a gradual and hereditary evil, which, when accompanied by general mendicity, ultimately operates with certain and baleful influence; the discontent, divisions, and hereditary enmities existing in all Mahomedan families where the offspring of several mothers have been matured, leads to destructive feuds, that greatly militate against the fruitful increase of the community. The administration of justice embodies an oppressive system of persecution, that produces mendicity and want, and consequent waste of life, for bread is the staff thereof. Other causes still more rife in the havoc of the human race, but which the general nature of these remarks does not elicit, tend inevitably and incontestably to unpeople the Mahomedan world. The plague annually extends its devastating hand over a blasted race, and the charnel battlefield of Moslem bigotry has been a dreadful scourge to the masses of the Turkish empire. There is no doubt that the rapid decrease of population, the rebellion of tributary provinces, and civil war, will shortly leave the Ottoman empire without efficient resources; and the government which borrows money at an interest of nine per cent, as the Turks are doing to pay the dividends of antecedent loans, has anticipated its means, and must finally and speedily be paralysed by the failure of nutrition.

The chief revenue of Oriental nations is derived from agricultural labour, and agriculture can only be fully elaborated by irrigation. The apocalyptic symbol of the Mahomedan empire is represented by "the great river Euphrates," and it is probable the drying up of the great river Euphrates, which all interpreters of prophecy agree means the Moslem power, points to the present fiscal perplexity of the Turkish government, in consequence of a deficient agrarian revenue, occasioned in a great degree by the gradual decrease of the population, which is disappearing, man by man, like the drying up of a stream silently and drop by drop exhaled : it is a fitting and appropriate symbol of approaching ruin. These are the main causes of decay perceptible in the Turkish power, and must determine its final dissolution, probably within a very short period.

Traditions are current amongst the Mahomedan nations of the East, (which are probably derived from our sacred books,) distinctly alluding to the national characteristics of the western race as the conquerors of the world. They believe in the advent of Christ, previous to which they are instructed to look for the appearance of the last of the Immaums.

This person, they say, is now, and has been for ages in existence; but owing to obstacles interposed by the immaturity of time, the desirable event is deferred to a future period. The appearance of Immaum Meihdee, as the personage is designated, must be preceded by several signs,—an infidel of monstrous form and dimensions, a frightful being of immense stature, with one eye, known by the name of Dijaul, is to devastate the earth, and destroy the faithful in great numbers. All Mahomedan communities are to become subject to Christian sway. The city of Bulkh (the ancient Bactra,) is to be rebuilt and flourish as the capital of Central Asia. There are also many others. When Islam shall become almost extinct, and in point of proportion to its former prevalence, resemble the size of a white spot on the forehead of a red cow, and Dijaul shall sorely distress the faithful, the Immaum will appear, fight with the infidel, and be nearly overcome in the contest; but the prospect of defeat will be speedily changed to the certainty of glorious victory by the advent of Christ, who must descend upon the roof of the temple of Mecca. He assists the Immaum, restores the fortune of battle, slays Dijaul, and converts all the world to Islam, i. e., the religion of peace. Thus we have Christ again bringing into the world peace and good-will to man. The Mahomedans say, " Christ will convert the world to their faith," but the book of traditions uses the term Islam, which, though it also signifies Mahomedanism, in a more extended application and literal sense means the religion of peace, and of this persuasion, say they, were the Patriarchs and all the Prophets; upon this point Moslem and Christian may agree. The first part of this tradition is near being accomplished. I have heard the Prince of Cabul remark, (in 1837,) "all the Mahomedan world is at this moment subject to Christian sway, except Cabul and Bocharah; when we are conquered the Immaum must appear." A year after this, Cabul was subdued by the English, and the prince a refugee in the States of Bocharah.

The principalities of the Uzbeck States are now the only Mahomedan powers not subject to Christian policy; but as Russia has offensive and defensive treaties with these Uzbecks of Tatary, and they are commercially and geographically connected with each other, a pretext will probably not long be wanting to enable Russia to plant the seeds of her policy there, as she has done in Persia and all the other Mahomedan communities of Central Asia. The people of Cabul consoled themselves upon the subjugation of their country, with the remark that the advent of the Immaum could not now be far off; and at his appearance, the faith and liberty of the Mosleman would again flourish and prosper. The unsettled state of oriental governments has latterly stimulated impostors to assume the name of Immaum Meihdee, and the pretensions of any individual arrogating the character are readily accredited by the wonder-loving crowds with surprising facility. I have frequently explained to pious Mahomedans the story of Dijaul, as an allegory of ignorance which is to pervade the world, before the manifestation of their Immaum, and the subsequent advent of the *Saviour*, as he is literally to prove in the midst of threatened defeat, dishonour, and death. A being monstrous in form, partially blind, an oppressive tyrant, and an unbeliever in revealed religion, pervading the universe, may be an appropriate figure of that desolating demon *Ignorance*. This negative principle is alone an adequate cause of the irreligion, and the evil polity, of the cruelty, rebellion, and oppression, to fill the world at the period of Christ's advent, as our Saviour himself has said, " nevertheless, when the Son of Man cometh, shall he find faith on the earth ?" The Mosleman generally refer with confidence to the coming of Dijaul, and suppose the allusion to this infidel is to be understood literally, though those to whom I offered an allegorical elucidation received the inference with an air of approving admiration.

At this moment the Moslem world regard with intense interest the near approach of Christ's advent—the divine being termed in the Koran " Soul of God"*—who is to bring peace (Islam) and good-will upon earth; and the Christian mind is prepared to hope from the signs of the times for the speedy appearance of Christ, to restore true religion to the world, to heal the afflictions of man, to establish the mercy of God upon earth, to bless all the human race, and *to execute judgment.* —" Blessing, and glory, and wisdom, and thanksgiving and honour, and power, and might, be unto our God for ever and ever"—(Rev. vii. 12.) There can be no question of the decay now progressing in the Ottoman empire. It has been verging towards dissolution many centuries. Fifty years ago, Volney, that famous infidel traveller in the East, expressed and proved the truth of this event, which is now rapidly advancing and is within the probable incidents of daily expectation. It is a consumma-

---

* Christ is the Soul of God.

tion which every Christian should devoutly pray for, as a forerunner of the Saviour's manifestation. 180,000,000 Mahomedans number amongst the articles of their faith, the advent of Christ, and anticipate with zealous enthusiasm the completion of their hope. Amongst the 200,000,000 Christians who inhabit the globe, how mysteriously supine are the minds of almost all who profess to believe in the vicarious promise of salvation, although *not* to understand appertaineth unto the wicked, whilst the wise shall understand, " and they that *be* wise shall shine as the brightness of the firmament, and they that turn many to righteousness as the stars for ever and ever"— Dan. xii. 3.—Mahomedan tradition and Christian faith unite in the belief of this important event. We mean not to impute the divine light of inspiration to the Mosleman where their traditions are purely original—but as I observed, these traditions are probably derived from some distorted relation of the oral accounts concerning Christ's second advent, prevalent in the church during the earliest age of its existence. If the 'time of the end is at hand; if the dissolution of the Mahomedan empire is about to result from the evident causes enumerated; if we are soon to witness the downfall of that power to " whom a host was given against the daily sacrifice by reason of transgression," and which has heretofore cast down the truth to the ground, and practised, and prospered, to whom power was given to take peace from the earth; of whom it is written, " yet he shall come to his end, and *none* shall help him"—no! though all the powers of earth combine to preserve the integrity of the Mahomedan empire, the *dissolution* of that empire shall be accomplished, and the word of God, which passeth not away, shall speedily be made manifest in the regeneration of man; if then, the time now is, when we can understand Mahomedanism to be expiring, we should turn again to Dan. xii. 1, and see that " At *that time* (when he shall come to his end) shall Michael stand up, the great prince which standeth for the children of thy people, and there shall be a time of trouble, such as never was since there was a nation even to that same time, and at *that time* thy people shall be delivered every one that shall be found written in the book," and Rev. xvi. 12, " And the sixth angel poured out his vial upon the great river Euphrates, and the water thereof was dried up, that the way of *the Kings of the East, might be prepared*," i. e., the reorganization of the Mahomedan empire, under Christian dynasties. And instantly it is said, calling our attention to the then present state of the world, verse 15 : " Behold I come as a thief; *blessed* is he that watcheth," and in contemporaneous sense it is added " and he gathered them together in a place called in the Hebrew tongue Armageddon."

When Constantinople shall be without a Moslem master, or the integrity of the Ottoman empire can no longer be maintained, a new arrangement must be made with the elements of the Mahomedan dominion. The existence of the British empire depends upon her paramount power as a maritime nation; and the aggrandizement of Russia by the fruition of her policy, which has occupied through ages the diplomacy of her government. The establishment of her hierarchy, and the construction of a maritime power stimulate Russia to the possession of Constantinople. By including this capital within her dominions, Russia gains egress through the Dardanelles for a fleet, and her armies and navies could impinge at once upon the south of Europe, whilst St. Petersburgh preserved her grasp upon the North; a position which would enable her to supersede England, and hold the balance of power in Europe. France demands Egypt. England also essentially requires she should hold it, to ensure undisturbed access to and safety of her Indian dominions. In short, the interests of England demand that she should rule over Constantinople and Egypt; whilst the interests of Russia require at least Constantinople, and France the annexation of Egypt with her dominion. How shall these conflicting interests be reconciled, and the stormy elements of war assuaged; it is probable they will be gathered together at Armageddon, *i. e.*, involved in bloody contention; because it is said, "At that time, (the time of the dissolution of the Ottoman empire,) shall Michael stand up, the great prince which standeth for the children of thy people, and there shall be a time of trouble, such as never was since there was a nation, even to that same time." Then the seventh angel shall sound, and confusion, war, and death rage through the world as the earth's foundations tremble at the trumpet's reverberation. But as the Jews will probably be reestablished in Jerusalem before the general war predicted, we may suppose that a congress of the five great European powers will quickly proceed to establish independent kingdoms of the wreck of the Ottoman empire, and place them, like Greece, under Christian dynasties, and these newly-arranged kingdoms will be under the patronage of a European diet or congress, until the time of the end, and the angel, which we have seen has been so long rising in the East, shall have accomplished his mission, which refers to the reorganization of the Jewish nation. Then the four angels standing on the four corners of the earth, no longer stayed in judgment, shall develope the final scene of strife and ultimate happiness of the human race, " when lo, a great multitude, which no man could number, of all nations, and kindred, and people, and tongues, stood before the throne, and before the Lamb, clothed with white robes and palms in their hands." Rev. vii. 9.

It is an incident worthy of remark, that the portending event of the Jews' restoration is entrusted to the protection and support of Michael, the great prince, who standeth for their nation. This name, as the Russians have the chief part to act, may refer to the commander-in-chief of the Russian armies, and point to Michael the Grand Duke, (great prince,) the emperor's brother; or it may refer to his imperial majesty's son of the same name, title, and designation. Michael, when mentioned in Scripture, is supposed to signify an archangel; that may be true, yet no inconsistency implicating the design of prophecy would be suggested by the hypothesis that the name means, in this instance, Michael the Grand Duke (of Russia). The time now is when those who run may read. There is a great running to and fro, and knowledge has increased to an extent never before known to the world; events characterizing the present age, and connecting it with the days of Daniel,—a great revolution, affecting the social and religious condition of the human race, the eternal salvation of mankind, is about to take place, " and blessed is he that watcheth," for " behold, I come as a thief."

III.

EXPLANATORY OF THE MAP.

Dreadful intelligence from Cabul.—Entire destruction of the British Cabul forces.—One European escaped.*

Bombay, March 1.

Advices from Bombay to the 1st inst. mention that the British troops, under a convention with Akhbar Khan, chief of the rebels, quitted their encampment on the 6th of January, and immediately after were engaged by the rebels, their rear being first attacked. In the course of three or four days, in which communications were carried on with the Chief, and the ladies given up, as well as several officers as hostages, the troops were fiercely engaged, the Chief pretending that he could not restrain them. Finally the sepoys succumbed, then Her Majesty's 44th. All ranks rushed towards Jellalabad, but only one European reached that city.

The news from Jellalabad is more cheering. General Sale's position has not been attacked. They have provisions enough till April. Reinforcements are expected to arrive in February.

AVGHANISTAUN.

The following letter from our correspondent in Bombay will be found to supply full details of the melancholy reverses our arms had sustained beyond the Indus. The letter is dated March 1, and brings

* From the London Times of April 4th, 1842.

down the narrative of events to the departure of the mail:

"The insurrection, which is described as participating in a great measure of the religious enthusiasm to which the fanatical Moslems can be excited by the preaching of their Imauns, broke out on the night of the 1st of November, when Sir Alexander Burnes, and his brother, and Captain Broadfoot of the 44th were killed; the house of the first named being within the city, was plundered; and some money in the treasury of Captain Johnson, which was close to the former house, was made a prey of. The captain having slept in the British cantonments, escaped the slaughter, as well as Brigadier Anquetil and Captain Troup, who were his inmates. Captains Skinner and Drummond, Captain Trevor and his lady and his children remained for some days concealed in the city by some of their friends.

"Shah Soojah, who had on the 2d sent his son to the relief of Sir Alexander Burnes, where the Prince performed prodigies of valour, received on that day a communication from Sir W. H. M'Naghten, then in the cantonment, about five miles from the town, requesting leave for Brigadier-General Skelton with two regiments, and Captain Nicholl's troop, to enter the Balla Hissar, and to shell the town. Leave was given, and the shelling took place. The infuriated populace attacked the Commissariat Fort, which lay immediately to the north of the town, between it and the cantonment, and as it was weakly defended, soon became masters of it. This was a dreadful blow to the troops, as at the time there was flour but for two days remaining in the cantonment. Another fort, in which some commissariat stores were kept was also attacked, and after a defence of three days by Captain Mackenzie, and a few men taken also, a panic appeared to have seized the troops, who found themselves in the beginning of winter shut up in their cantonments in a valley 200 miles from the Indus, without sufficient clothing or food, and amidst a fanatical Mussulman population. Even between the British leaders a difference of opinion prevailed: the Envoy being desirous of offensive measures, while General Elphinstone, from circumstances connected with the forces, among whom despondency and vacillation are described as then prevailing, maintained his opinion for defensive ones. At the solicitation of the Envoy, some small forts in the neighbourhood, which contained grain, were captured. In the meantime the news of the dispersion of several of the Affghan corps in Shah Soojah's service, commanded by British officers, reached the besieged, and contributed to add to their gloomy prognostics. Various reverses and successes followed during some days. The troops from the Balla Hissar were recalled to the Cantonment, and the Envoy urged a decided attack on the enemy; the General, however, maintained that all such attacks would be futile: the soldiers began to despond, and all was misery. There were, nevertheless, skirmishes every day, which did not tend to raise the spirits of the sepoys and soldiers, who saw their enemy hourly increase, while they themselves had scarcely food and but insufficient raiment for the season. So greatly were they dispirited that they were one day driven back to their camp, after they had during three hours been exposed to a galling fire. The Ghilzee Chief Osman Khan did not choose to pursue them within their entrenchments, where they, it was then feared, would have made a feeble resistance. Their provision was flour, which they obtained by bribery during the night. It was then recommended that all the troops should be concentrated in the Balla Hissar. Captain Conolly, who was then with the Shah, advocated the propriety of so doing, but the military authorities declared the movement impossible, as they could not rely upon the disheartened troops. The last regiment was then withdrawn from the Balla Hissar, which is, as every one knows, a citadel on a hill to the eastward of the town, and Shah Soojah was left to his own resources.

" The insurgents, who were aware of the movement of succour from Candahar, now appeared disposed to enter upon negotiations for the withdrawal of the British troops. The envoy, on hearing of the retreat of the Candahar brigade, and learning that no aid could be expected from General Sale, then at Jellalabad, or from the Indus, gave a reluctant assent. Conferences took place, and a long list of articles, drawn up in Persian by Sir W. H. M'Naghten, was agreed to on both sides. They are said to exceed twenty in number.

" The second and favourite son of Dost Mahomed, Mahomed Akhbar Khan, who, subsequent to his father's surrender had remained in concealment, and had even escaped beyond the confines of Avghanistaun, having made his appearance during the insurrection, took a decided part in the negotiation. The insurgent chiefs exhibited great willingness to have the British troops removed from Cabul, and arrangements are said to have been made for that purpose at different meetings which were held outside the cantonments. After various parleys, a message was, on the 22d of December, brought from

Akhbar Khan to Sir W. H. M'Naghten, to request an interview on the following morning. The British envoy went thither, accompanied by Captains Lawrence, Trevor, and Mackenzie. They had not been present five minutes, when a signal was given and all were seized and forced to mount behind some Ghilzee chiefs. The British envoy resisted, and was slain, as also Captain Trevor, who had slipped off the horse on which he had been placed. Their murderers are now said to be "Ghazees," or religious enthusiasts, who fight as soldiers for "the sake of God," and who, if killed in battle, are called "Shuhdees," or martyrs. The treatment of Sir W. H. M'Naghten's body has been described as most barbarous. His lady is stated to have offered a large sum for its ransom, in order to its being decently interred. The other two officers were saved by the dread of the Ghazees to fire at them, lest the Ghilzees, who rode before them should be wounded; they returned to the cantonment on the 28th. Akhbar Khan has, it appears, boasted of his having in person killed Sir W. H. M'Naghten.

"Major Pottinger, well known since the defence of Herat, took charge of the British mission, and the negotiations for the withdrawal of the troops were continued. On the 6th of January they moved from their cantonments, which were instantly seized by the insurgents and burnt. The snow was one foot deep on the ground, when the troops reached Bèegrom, three miles distant. The schemes of Akhbar Khan then became evident: he had despatched emissaries throughout the country through which the unfortunate British soldiers had to pass, calling on the people to rise *en masse* and slay the infidels. His call was not heard in vain. On the first day's march Cornet Hardyman, of the 5th cavalry, and some men were killed. Mahomed Akhbar Khan, who had taken charge of the retreat, contrived to induce the British to take up stations at night where he chose. On the 7th they moved to Bareckhar, where the three mountain guns were seized. Their rear guard were obliged to act on the defensive during the whole of the day. On the 8th the camp was nearly surrounded by enemies, and it became evident that the British troops would have to fight their way to Jellalabad. Captain Skinner went to Mahomed Akhbar Khan, who was on a hill close to the British camp, and inquired why they could not proceed according to the convention. The reply was that they had left the Cabul cantonments before the troops destined to protect them were ready, and that no chief but he (Akhbar Khan) had the means or power to protect them, notwithstanding their convention.

" This military convention is not fully known, and therefore all its provisions cannot be stated. It is pretended that among the articles there are some declaring, that all the British troops were to evacuate Avghanistaun, and that notice of such a convention had been sent to General Nott at Candahar, and to General Sale at Jellalabad. It is said to have been signed by General Elphinstone as Commander in Chief, and by Major Pottinger as acting Political Agent, and also by Brigadier Skelton, Brigadier Anquetil, and Colonel Chambers.

"Akhbar Khan, whose violent hatred to the British had been sharpened, not only by the conquest of his father's territories, but by his own exile and subsequent imprisonment in Bokhara, and by his wild fanaticism, demanded then, on the third day of the retreat from Cabul, that the British should, when surrounded by the Ghazees under his command, make new terms with him, and promise not to proceed farther than Tazeen, until the withdrawal of the force under Sir R. Sale from Jellalabad, was known, and he insisted on six hostages. Major Pottinger, who was lame from a wound, instantly offered to be one, and at Akhbar Khan's orders Captains M'Kenzie and Lawrence were included. The Ghazees were, however, not restrained in their attacks, and a fearful slaughter followed on the movement towards Khoord Cabul. The column was attacked on all sides. The fourteen ladies, who were in the centre, seemed objects of special desire. Mrs. Anderson and Mrs. Boyd had each a child carried off. Akhbar Khan, while the Ghazees were thus busy, professed his inability to restrain them, and on the 9th of January demanded that the ladies should be placed under his protection. The miserable weather, the snowy wastes, the rough mountain tracks, and the month of January in the coldest regions of Central Asia, compelled them to yield: the hostages halted for some days in that neighbourhood.

"The demand on General Sale to relinquish his post was made on the 9th of January, and on that day he refused to do so, unless by orders from the Supreme Government. This answer was taken back to Akhbar Khan. The unfortunate sepoys began again to move, and were again assailed; the sepoys, who form such good soldiers under the broiling sun of India, being enervated and stupified by the cold, scarcely offered any resistance, and hundreds of them were soon despatched by the Ghazee cutthroats, but the Europeans and some brave men kept together until they reached the pass of Jugdulluk. Here General Elphinstone and Brigadier Skelton became hostages, and were detained two miles distant by Akhbar. General Elphinstone wrote a note in pencil to Brigadier Anquetil— 'March to-night; there is treachery.' The British troops marched early in the night; they came to the frightful mountain pass; it was barricadoed; they forced the way, and reached Jugdulluk, which they defended some time, until Brigadier Anquetil was killed. All order was then lost, and confusion and separation, slaughter and destruction ensued. Several officers who were well mounted attempted to make good their way into Jellalabad. Some of them arrived within three or four miles, when they were murdered and plundered, and their bodies left on the road. Only one officer, Doctor Brydon, of the 5th Bengal Native Infantry, though wounded in several places, and exhausted, succeeded in reaching the place of safety in Jellalabad on the 13th. Of the fate of the other 4,000 soldiers and 6,000 camp followers nothing certain is known; many have been killed, others are dispersed, and as yet it is difficult to decide. The names of thirty-five officers have been published as killed from the commencement of the insurrection, but fears are entertained that they may amount to its quadruple, out of the great number missing. Some of the sepoys are said to have been sold as slaves to the Oosbeg Tartars.

" Letters continue to arrive from various quarters representing the state of the prisoners and hostages. Akhbar Khan is said in a letter received from Major Pottinger, dated January 23d, to be at the fort of Badeeabad, in the Lughman country, where he keeps the following prisoners, viz.:—General Elphinstone and Skelton, Lieutenant Mac Kenzie, Captain and Mrs. Anderson and child, Captain Boyd, Lieutenant Eye, Lieutenant Waller, Mrs. Trevor, Lady Sale, Lady Macnaghten, Mrs. Sturt, Mr. and Mrs. Ryley, Sergeant and Mrs. Wade, Captains Troop, Johnson, and G. P. Lawrence, and Major Pottinger. There are besides, the six officers and the sick who were left at Cabul on the departure of the troops. Akhbar Khan, in the letters from that fort, which are received unsealed, is described as doing every thing " to make them comfortable!"

"An attempt of the insurgents to seize Ghuznee is said to be so far successful as that the town is in their power, but Colonel Palmer, with his regiment and six months' provision is stated to be safe in the citadel. At Candahar an insurgent force showed itself on the 10th of January, when an attempt was made to carry off the camels belonging to the 43d Bengal Native Infantry. On the 11th, Prince Sufter Jung, the youngest and favourite son of Shah Sooja, and Mahomed Atta, the Chief, came with a large force within about five miles' distance. General Nott marched against them on the 12th, and in a short time dispersed the whole with a trifling loss; the young Prince proved himself a coward, as he is a traitor to his father's friends.

" General Sale has, however, maintained his position at Jellalabad, which he had fortified with a ditch, and planted cannon in different places, with a determination to defend his position to the utmost. Akhbar Khan has attempted to raise the Oolooses, or heads of the neighbouring clans, in order to attack Jellalabad, but the gallantry and resolution displayed by Sir Robert Sale in October, during his march from Cabul to Jellalabad, had given them such proofs of his bravery that they have hitherto rather hesitated. The troops in Jellalabad are stated to be well provided with food and able to keep their ground until the beginning of March, particularly since they have already discomfited two contemplated attacks.

"The celebrated mountain pass, called the Khyber, lies between Jellalabad and Peshawar, and the inhabitants, who are in possession, have been long notorious for their plundering propensities. Akhbar Khan sent to offer money to induce them to resist not only the departure of the troops under General Sale, but also the entry of all the troops which may be ordered by the Supreme Government to relieve the garrison at Jellalabad. The Khyberries are stated to be highly incensed at the small sum offered for their concurrence in his plans by Akhbar Khan. It was not more than 1,500 rupees. They, however, have made preparations to resist on their own account, and a brigade, under the command of Colonel Wild, which was sent from the Sutledge early in December, having reached Peshawar, made an attempt to force the pass. Having left their artillery behind in India, and the only guns procurable in that direction being unserviceable ones from the Seikhs, the attempt made by Colonel Wild was unsuccessful. Two regiments penetrated to the fort of Ali Musjid, where a British garrison was stationed; but, as they found neither provisions nor ammunition there, they were obliged to retreat towards Peshawar, having lost an officer and some men. In the meantime the Supreme Government has not been idle. General

Pollock has been despatched at the head of a considerable reinforcement towards Peshawar, which he with sufficient guns and abundant ammunition reached on the 7th ult., and is now making preparations for proceeding through the Khytar pass.

"The Supreme Government on the 31st of January published a proclamation admitting the fact of the convention at Cabul, the retreat of the troops, and their having suffered extreme disaster in consequence of treacherous attacks, and declaring that the most active measures had been adopted, and would be most steadily pursued, for expediting powerful reinforcements to the Avghan frontier for assisting such operations as may be considered necessary for the maintenance of the honour and interest of the British Government in that quarter.

"Orders were also published on the 5th of February for the purpose of having a 10th company added to every regiment in India, which, with other measures adopted, will cause an increase of about 26,000 men.

"The latest intelligence from Cabul is, that Shah Soojah has succeeded in securing the good-will of all the chiefs. Newab Mahomed Zeman Khan has been appointed Vizier, and Ameer Oolla Lagharee, and one of the leaders in the late insurrection, has been named Ameer-ud-Dowla. Akhbar Khan, has no power now in Cabul, and was sent to attend the "Feringees" in their retreat in order to get rid of him. He, however, retains the hostages and prisoners, for whom he is likely to demand a large ransom. His father, Dost Mahomed, is strongly guarded, in order to prevent his escape from India. There is great talk of "our great friend" Shah Soojah-ool-Molk being implicated in the late insurrection, which appears to have been exclusively directed against the foreign infidels."

Extract of a letter from a gentleman in Northern India to his friends in Philadelphia.

"January 17th, 1842.

" In this country the power of the British Company was considered absolute. The honour of God was a thing unthought of, and if thought of, only remembered to be despised. The Sabbath day was dishonoured by all classes of men, from the Governor-General to the lowest soldier: the people were living and dying in ignorance of the true God, and the rulers set their faces as brass against all efforts to Christianize the nation. They felt themselves strong without God—they needed not that he should direct them—they had conquered, and were reaping vast riches from the people, and they thought they would extend their conquests. Mark the result—they planned an Avghan war—they marched into the country, with scarcely any opposition, when had a thousand rifles taken possession of the mountain passes, they could not have set their feet in that country. The Lord allowed them to go in and set themselves down. Depending on their own strength they felt themselves secure; they thought of sending home some of the troops, and lo! when they thought they had by their own arms accomplished a great victory, they find themselves surrounded by countless warlike men, many of whom will take their heart's blood rather than surrender their land to Christians; and now, they have got into difficulty, how shall they get out? With thousands of soldiers, they are nevertheless afraid to put their noses outside their entrenched camp; they are short of provisions, and owing to the climate and nature of the country, they cannot for some time to come, obtain assistance from the provinces. There they are, they went of their own accord. How they will get out, or what they will do time alone will make manifest. Of one fact we are certain—the glory of God, and extension of his cause formed no part of the object of the undertaking. Some Christian officers who were anxious to distribute Scriptures and tracts were severely threatened with the displeasure of their superiors, if they did not cease from their endeavours to Christianize the people!"

References explanatory of the Map of Djillalabad, referred to in Appendix I., p. 176.

A. Cabul gate of Djillalabad.

B C. Forts held by enemy—C being Azeez Khan's headquarters.

E E E. Ruined forts held by enemy.

G 1 and G 2. Portions of Abbott's guns advancing. The dotted line with arrows shows retreat of enemy's columns, which were nearly all obliged to recross the river.

THE END.

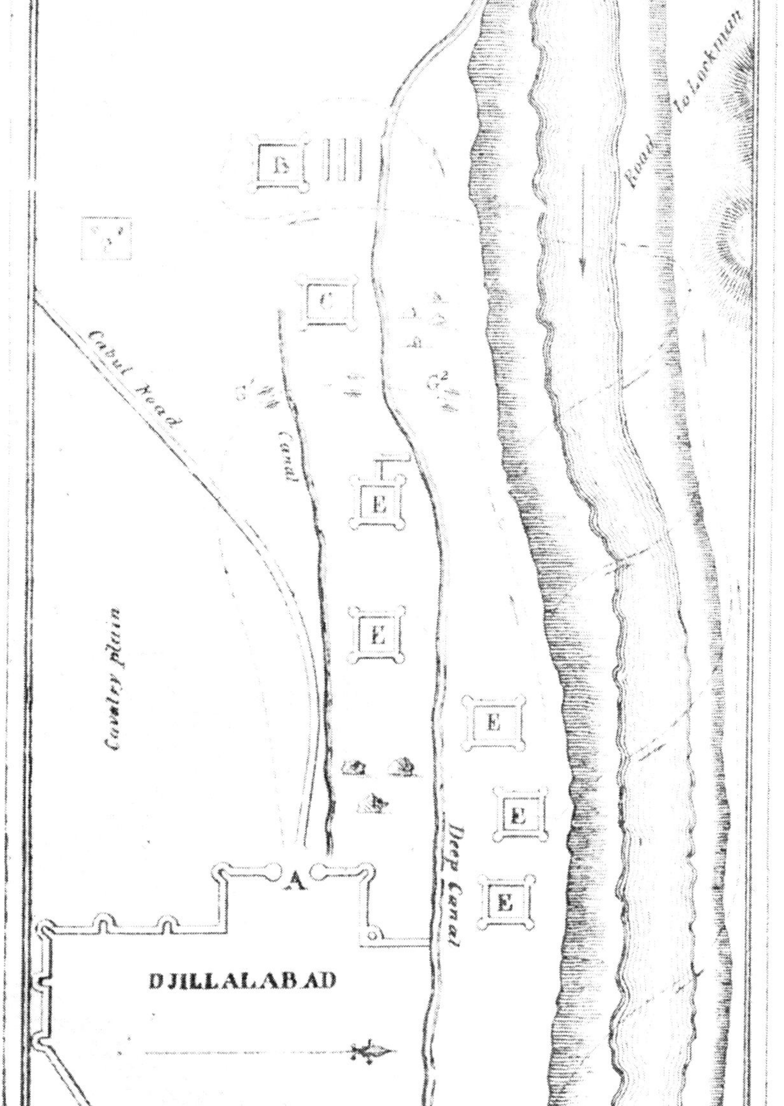

DJILLALABAD
A
B
C
E
E
E
E
E
E
G
Cabul Road
Canal
Deep Canal
Cavalry plain
Road to Lockman

A. Carnn engf

Made in the USA
Lexington, KY
05 August 2011